# Land, Liberation, and Death Squads

# Land, Liberation, and Death Squads

*A Priest's Story*
*Suchitoto, El Salvador, 1968–1977*

## José Inocencio Alas

Foreword by Joaquín E. Garay

Translated by Robin Fazio and Emily Wade Will

RESOURCE *Publications* · Eugene, Oregon

LAND, LIBERATION, AND DEATH SQUADS
A Priest's Story, Suchitoto, El Salvador, 1968–1977

Copyright © 2016 José Inocencio Alas. All rights reserved. Except for brief quotations in critical publications or reviews, no part of this book may be reproduced in any manner without prior written permission from the publisher. Write: Permissions, Wipf and Stock Publishers, 199 W. 8th Ave., Suite 3, Eugene, OR 97401.

Resource Publications
An Imprint of Wipf and Stock Publishers
199 W. 8th Ave., Suite 3
Eugene, OR 97401

www.wipfandstock.com

PAPERBACK ISBN: 978-1-4982-9225-2
HARDCOVER ISBN: 978-1-4982-9227-6
EBOOK ISBN: 978-1-4982-9226-9

Manufactured in the U.S.A.                                                 JANUARY 5, 2017

Cornell Capa © International Center of Photography/Magnum Photos

An English translation of *Iglesia, Tierra y Lucha Campesina*

To the memory of my mother, Cayetana de Jesús Gómez de Alas,
Monsignor Luis Chávez y González, Monsignor Óscar Romero,
and the martyrs of Suchitoto.

I thought of the campesinos for whom I had struggled in these last months of my life. I was content to be able to suffer for them, to share their destiny; they are society's eternally oppressed and scorned. I thought about their land, which for them is life. To die as a martyr is to succeed in having one's message escape one's body and run through the world sowing winds of hope.

CHENCHO ALAS

# Contents

*Foreword by Joaquín E. Garay* | *ix*
*Acknowledgments* | *xiii*
*Introduction* | *xv*

| | |
|---|---|
| Chapter 1 | The Beginning of a Struggle \| 1 |
| Chapter 2 | Theological Sources of the Suchitoto Ministry \| 16 |
| Chapter 3 | A Demonstration in San Salvador \| 26 |
| Chapter 4 | Forging Community Leaders \| 35 |
| Chapter 5 | Land for the Campesinos and Genuine Christian Conversion \| 52 |
| Chapter 6 | Kidnapped \| 62 |
| Chapter 7 | The Monsignor Luis Chávez y González School of Agriculture \| 81 |
| Chapter 8 | The Capture of Thirty-Seven ANDES Teachers \| 90 |
| Chapter 9 | Presidential Elections \| 95 |
| Chapter 10 | The Cerrón Grande Dam \| 100 |
| Chapter 11 | 1974 Elections \| 116 |
| Chapter 12 | The Unified Popular Action Front \| 130 |
| Chapter 13 | Suchitoto: Cradle of Emerging Values \| 137 |
| Chapter 14 | Repression Intensifies throughout the Whole Country \| 144 |

CONTENTS

Chapter 15    Monsignor Romero | 154
Chapter 16    My Last Days in El Salvador | 169
Chapter 17    Thirty Years Later | 177

*Bibliography* | *187*

# Foreword

"It was two o'clock in the afternoon on the first Sunday of April 1969." With these words José Inocencio Alas, known as Chencho Alas, begins his book. In it he recounts his memories of the period he worked as a priest of the San Salvador Archdiocese, serving as parish priest of Suchitoto and its thirty cantons from 1969 until his departure into exile on May 25, 1977. He worked in the parish with his brother, Higinio Alas; in 1971 they were joined by Fathers Jesus Bengoechea, SJ, and Bernardo Boulang. As Chencho himself explains, this book does not attempt "a systematic analysis of our Suchitoto ministry." Rather, "it consists solely of memories of events that illustrate our ministry and its relationship to the land issue."

*Memories of events.* Alas provides an introduction and interpretation of the background to El Salvador's armed conflict, especially between 1969 and 1975.

*Events that illustrate our ministry and its relationship to the land issue.* Chencho Alas's analysis leads him to say that the conflict's origin lies in the catastrophic consequences of El Salvador's land tenure system for poor campesinos.[1] "Our country's land problem permitted the development of a prewar dynamic that served as a trigger for a wide range of values, problems, struggles, and aspirations."

In narrative form and a fresh, straightforward style, he guides the reader through geography and time to the years of his ministry. A concrete event like the conflict at the Aguas Calientes Hacienda spurs his motivation to accompany the poor in their struggles for rights as a direct demand of his

---

1. *Campesino* may be translated as "peasant farmer."

evangelical efforts. From then on this commitment becomes, in Suchitoto parish, a requirement of Christian faith.

He relates how his pastoral ministry was transformed in trying to give concrete responses to concrete situations: the events surrounding the La Asunción hacienda, campesino demonstrations, the growth and expansion of organizations like FECCAS, the challenges facing the first agrarian reform and the "curulazo"[2] of 1970, the conflict over CEL's construction of the Cerrón Grande Dam and its impact on campesino families in the area, and other happenings. He also recounts the beginnings of systematic repression, the formation of ORDEN, and the dreadful death squads that caused so much mourning in innumerable Salvadoran families.

The author speaks of the ministry of some of the diocesan priests of the San Salvador archdiocese, his friendship with Father Rutilio Grande, his pastoral choices and motivations, and his understanding of evangelization and the church's mission in the period when it was applying Vatican II and Medellín's conclusions to its work.

The book is intended as a testimony to the work and personality of Monsignor Chávez y González: his openness and intuition made him a visionary. His zeal for pastoral work was continued and carried to its fullest expression by his successor, Monsignor Óscar Arnulfo Romero. It equally recognizes those Salvadoran diocesan clergy who applied the best of Latin American theological reflections and committed themselves to the poor, while dreaming of transforming the county's culture of death. Many of them shed their blood or went into exile.

Chencho Alas studied philosophy in the San José de La Montaña seminary and later had the opportunity to continue his studies abroad to prepare for the priesthood: in Sherbrooke, Canada; in the Pontifical Gregorian University of Rome; at the International Lumen Vitae Institute in Brussels, Belgium; and in the Latin American Pastoral Institute in Quito, Ecuador, where he received the motivational boost for his work in Suchitoto.

His experience allows him to analyze the economic, historical, and cultural reality of the Salvadoran people. His closeness to the campesinos, with their concrete views of the universe, led him to theological reflection of baptism and its link to issues such as land reform, grace-sin-liberation,

---

2. The *"curulazo"* refers to the unexpected calling for a conference on agrarian reform in 1970 by Dr. Juan Gregorio Guardado, president of the National Assembly. Guardado took this measure without first consulting or getting approval from the country's president. (The Spanish *curul* refers to a parliament seat and the suffix *-azo* means "a blow" or "hit.")

the meaning of the concept of God's people, of the priesthood, and so forth. Deserving special mention are his memories of some of the people's martyrs and his opinion of specific turning points of Monsignor Romero's inner transformation, to which he dedicates one chapter.

To keep the narrative's close, conversational style, the author's stylistic expressions have been retained. Some repetition or diverging comments within a single chronicle are inevitable! It may seem obvious but it should be expressly noted that the presentation, content, and interpretations inherent in the subject matter are those of the author.

Criticism or possible repudiation by those who have a different interpretation of this era of the Salvadoran people's struggle is a given. But, obviously, even those sharing the same ideals may have differences of opinion, even disagreements, in the interpretation of issues such as the origins of Christian Base Communities or the Christian-inspired campesino organization in El Salvador. Chencho Alas himself alludes to the controversies of those who confronted him about his pastoral choices or about his specific strategies in regards to: his relationship with the popular political organizations who fought among themselves for hegemony of the political organizational work, his interpretation of "the first FAPU," the criticism he received for not agreeing with the view of deepening societal contradictions, and so forth.

The philosopher Walter Benjamin dedicated a good part of his academic efforts to the understanding of history; he died in exile fleeing the German Gestapo on September 25, 1940, in Port Bou of the Spanish Pyrenees. His tomb is inscribed with a phrase taken from his writings: "It is much more difficult to honor the memories of the Nameless than the famous. For that reason, historical construction should be mainly devoted to the Nameless."

We are in the era of electronic means of "artificial memory," of computer technology that is bringing about a true cultural revolution. The flood of information and the acceleration of daily life are causing a crisis in the new generations' sense of direction in such a way that the need to forget is claiming more weight than the need to remember and commemorate. Some people continue to propose forgetting, or worse, the total suppression of historical memory as a shield to avoid depression in the face of human catastrophes. Actually they intend to castrate the people's future.

This book is intended to be part of a series of publications in which direct witnesses of the history of the Salvadoran conflict "narrate" what happened: when, how, and where. The primary purpose is to try to support the preservation of historical memory so that this dense time of El Salvador's history becomes part of the collective cultural memory of future generations, with the firm hope that they will ritually remember the victims of this important time in our history and with the conviction that it will spark anew the search for justice, the dream of naming the "nameless": the poor who shed their blood for a more dignified, just, and Christian El Salvador.

Christian faith itself is based on the commemorative memory of the martyrdom and resurrection of Jesus Christ. Who better than we Christians should have a special sensitivity for the subject?

Joaquín E. Garay, OFM

# Acknowledgments

THANKS TO ROBERT SMITH for financing this book's translation and corrections. Special thanks to Ryne Clos for doing the editing pro bono and to Emily Wade Will for her assistance every time I needed it.

# Introduction

THE LAND ISSUE HAS been the Salvadoran people's historical challenge. The armed uprisings of the nineteenth and twentieth centuries had their origins in the wide disparity of land ownership. Land is not only "mother" for us all, but it also means bread for the poor and power for the rich, survival for the poor and comfort and luxury for those who have everything. The land is what's closest to life, and it is life for everyone.

I never imagined my ministry in Suchitoto parish would be so tied to the problem of land tenure! The following lines, written during fifteen years of exile and some of them after I returned to the country in 1992, are intended only to share the experiences lived with my co-workers: my brother Higinio, who accompanied me up to my last day among this dear people; the priest Tilo Sánchez, "a one of a kind," as the people have always said of him because of the way he faces his life's tasks; Father Bernardo Boulang, a Frenchman who above all tried to identify with our communities' problems, particularly those of the youth; Jorge Miranda, who carried out his priestly ministry at the beginning of the Suchitoto experience; and Father Jesús Ángel Bengoechea, a Jesuit who came to live with us for about a year, to experience in the flesh the realities of a rural parish.

This experience is particularly rich due to the input and active presence of the campesinos, especially the community leaders. Without them we could have done nothing; we would have been trees without fruit planted on the roadside of our dusty tropics. In truth, in Suchitoto, history is made by such martyrs as Toño Valte, Elías Acosta, Escamillita, and countless other campesinos and campesinas of our small villages. We have only

## INTRODUCTION

accompanied them in their tremendous fight for life, land, bread, justice, and peace.

The chapters that follow are not a systematic analysis of the pastoral work in Suchitoto. They are only memories of events that illustrate our ministry and its relationship to the land issue, an issue that still exists in the country and will cause new struggles in the near future. The flame of the land struggle has not died, its embers are smoking, and sooner or later, if there is no change in policy, our homes will once again ignite with more violence and the people who deserve better will again weep. El Salvador's churches face a huge task, and they cannot hide behind it with their apolitical statements. Church leaders may be fine with the government, the oligarchy, and the colonels, but not with Jesus of Nazareth, who from his town's synagogue proclaimed his mission citing Isaiah's words:

> The Spirit of the Lord is upon me,
> because he has anointed me
> to preach good news to the poor.
> He has sent me to heal the brokenhearted,
> to proclaim freedom to the captives,
> to restore sight to the blind,
> to deliver those who are oppressed,
> and to proclaim the year of the Lord . . .
> Today this scripture has been fulfilled and you yourselves are witnesses.
> Luke 4:18–19 and 21b

## Chapter 1

# The Beginning of a Struggle

It was two o'clock in the afternoon on the first Sunday of April 1969. I was resting, taking a nap. Sundays are overwhelming in a town parish, where the first mass starts at five o'clock in the morning. I was not used to such a pace because I had spent my life in seminaries, universities, and parishes in the capital.

At that hour, someone knocked on the door, and I got up to open it. Five campesinos from San Juan canton were waiting at the entrance. With little introduction, Don Moncho said, "They have taken away our land. This year we are not going to be able to plant our corn. Dr. Miguel Ángel Quiñónez, owner of Aguas Calientes Hacienda, has thrown us off his property. This year my family, my friends and their families, and I will starve. There are five of us without land. We overcame many difficulties to prepare it and now it is ready for the May planting."

I asked him why they had lost it and he replied, "We had signed a lease with Dr. Quiñónez giving us the right to use the land for a year. According to the contract, we had to clear the land and leave it clean so he could plant grass next year. We have done that, except for removing some tree trunks that are so thick and heavy we cannot pull them out even with a team of oxen. A tractor is needed, and we do not have one."

In El Salvador, landowners grant the use of land in different ways. Don Moncho and his four partners had signed a contract, a simple way in which the user pays a fee for the work he wants to do on the land or per land area. "Halves" is another method. As the name suggests, expenses and earnings are split in half. Another way is for tenant farmers to cultivate plots within a farm or hacienda. This arrangement most resembles what existed during colonial times: the tenant farmer is basically a servant whose unconditional labor was purchased by the landowner giving him a place to live and grow food crops as well as a meager wage.

I asked Moncho if the five heads of households had spoken with the doctor, and he said that they had, without favorable results. The reality was that customarily the doctor rented land to peasants, always for a one-year period. When the land was ready for planting, he took it away from some of the peasants, claiming different reasons. If the tenants refused, he went to the local court, where he was powerful enough to do what he pleased. Not for nothing was he the richest man in town. In this way he had been clearing his hacienda to plant pasture to expand the area he dedicated to cattle raising.

Dr. Quiñónez, who has since died, had a long family history. He was the nephew of Alfonso Quiñónez Molina, a physician from Suchitoto who was El Salvador's president from 1923 to 1927. His election was due to his affiliation with the conservative and criminal Meléndez dynasty. According to the *New York Times Magazine*, the Quiñónezes were members of the legendary Fourteen Families, who had dominated the country politically and economically.[1] This explains the power Dr. Quiñónez held in Suchitoto. He was very well connected with the powerful groups in San Salvador.

I listened carefully to Moncho. His words were sincere, and they illuminated a reality, the relationship between landowners and peasants, I did not know. Many times it would fall to me to listen to the campesinos, hear their complaints, their concerns, learn of their aspirations. They were my best school for getting to know my country's reality. The campesino's speech is simple and heartfelt, born of life and reality, and his or her ambitions are few. Campesinos want food for their children, education, health, land to grow their corn and beans, and a little house to shelter them.

The system, the existing structure, denies them these few things. To change it is not communism, it is simple humanism; to be able to count oneself among human beings is fundamental, basic, "the vital minimum," as the great Salvadoran essayist Alberto Masferrer said. According to Masferrer, a program offering safe and honest work; sufficient, varied, and nutritious food; adequate housing; health care and medical attention; prompt and honest justice; decent education; and rest and recreation are sufficient to guarantee the population's welfare. To these points he added the necessity of redistributing the land or agrarian reform.[2]

1. Hoeffel, "Eclipse of the Oligarchs."
2. For more on this, see Alberto Masferrer, "El minimum vital."

At five that afternoon, I said the last Sunday mass. I tried to root my preaching in the lectionary, the liturgical season, and current events published by the national press. That Sunday lent itself to denouncing Dr. Quinónez's evictions from his land and the system's legalized injustices. I specifically mentioned, without naming, the judge who with his verdicts had benefited the city's wealthy. One basic way of maintaining the status quo is the corruption of the judicial system. Judges easily sell themselves or simply rule in favor of those with political or economic power to avoid creating problems for themselves.

Because I was very new in Suchitoto at that time, I did not know the doctor's wife or the magistrate. After the liturgy, I greeted some people in the atrium. I realized there was a lady who was reluctant to approach me. Well-dressed and demure, she looked like a high-society woman with a svelte, dignified appearance. I approached her, and she said, "I listened to your sermon carefully. You referred to my husband when you mentioned the land issue. My husband is not a bad man nor is he interested in expanding his cattle grazing. He can do so without involving the peasants who reported him to you. What happens is that the peasants do not like him and do not fulfill the obligations they have incurred. They want everything the easy way." I tried to explain to the lady the campesinos' need to raise their corn and beans and the consequences for their families if they did not do so. She did not listen and walked away from me upset.

## Judge Cotto Opens a New Trial

I realized that an older man, very bald and cheerful, was listening to my conversation with the lady. After she moved away, he came over and said, "I am the justice of the peace, my name is Alfonso Cotto, and I am at your service." He extended his hand to me. "I have not committed any violation of the law in favoring Dr. Quiñónez. The campesinos did not comply with the agreement and I had to rule against them.

"However, so that you see I am an honest and fair man, I will reopen the case in two weeks. You will receive a notice from the court appointing you as the campesinos' 'good man' and I will name one for Dr. Quiñónez as well." The term "good man," *homo bonus*, was coined by Roman law. It refers to the person who during a trial intervenes with arguments in support of the accused. The judge evaluates both parties' arguments and then decides in favor of one of them. I immediately accepted his proposal.

The two weeks prior to the new trial were ones of intense activity for me. Immediately I told the affected peasants that the case would be opened again. They thanked me. Not knowing what to do, because of lack of experience in that field, I called Francisco Díaz, in his last year of law school, so he could advise me. Francisco had participated in the *cursillos de Cristiandad*[3] that I had founded in El Salvador during the period I worked with the Salvadoran upper class. He was always a man of social conscience, a just man, and a great gentleman.

Francisco came to Suchitoto and together we toured the doctor's estate, located on the banks of the Quezalapa River, a few kilometers from the city. A campesino accompanied us to check the status of the land they had cleared for cultivation. Francisco had suggested I bring a camera and take some photos and I had and did. The land had been burned in the way it was customarily done in the country; all that remained were tree trunks that, being freshly cut, had not burned. They were immense. A good tractor was needed to pull them out of the ground. As we examined the place, Francisco explained my role in the trial and let me know he was coming as a consultant, not a lawyer, and would not intervene much. Primarily, this was because he had not yet graduated.

Two weeks later, a Sunday, at two in the afternoon, the trial began in a room of the Suchitoto town hall. In the morning, I realized few campesino men had come to mass. Mainly women were at church. Toward noon, the city was flooded with men with serious faces, carrying their hats. The air in the city was hot, suffocating. Soon the rains would begin, perhaps in two weeks. The May rains bring freshness, flowers, and hope for a good harvest and bread for our poor people's tables. The rich always have their bread.

I arrived at the town hall at two on the dot; I always arrive on time in order to carry out my responsibilities. Francisco, who gave me the impression of being very nervous, accompanied me. He was still just a kid. The five peasants awaited me in the building's hallway. The judge invited us into a poorly furnished room where he had his office. There awaited his secretary, whom some might say was in a permanent state of alcoholic preservation. A calendar hung on the wall and a few chairs were scattered in the room.

---

3. Editor's Note: The term "cursillos de Cristiandad" approximately translates to "Christian short courses." They were employed widely throughout Latin America in the years after World War II and had many different variations and goals. Many were simply spiritual in nature and intended for Catholic revival, whereas others were quite sociopolitical and intended in part to raise the level of political consciousness of the parishioners who attended.

## THE BEGINNING OF A STRUGGLE

We were about to sit when Dr. Miguel Ángel Quiñónez, accompanied by his son, who studied law, and his "good man," Mr. Carlos Henríquez, also a landowner, arrived. The doctor was a tall man, well on in years, slightly stooped, dressed in white, and leaning on a lavishly carved cane. He appeared to me a tired man. In town, he was known as "*Macho Prieto*," because of his dark skin. He had served as the physician for generations of Suchitoto residents and the shadow under which most town politicians had found shelter.

The judge opened the trial with a short speech. In it, he asserted that his previous ruling was fair, but that, due to my public complaint in my sermon, he graciously saw fit to give a new opportunity to the peasants to have their "good man"—he pointed to me—defend their cause. He told us the rules of the game. The campesinos and the doctor had no right to speak, unless the judge asked them to. The "good men," who should already know their party's case, would present arguments in favor or against. This was my first time participating in something like this, the first time I found myself before a judge.

The judge asked me to begin with my statement because I was the most interested in the matter. I started by thanking the judge for showing interest in justice and for his kindness in bringing the case to a new trial. I spoke of the land's importance to the peasant farmers and about their having complied with the contract's clauses, insofar as was possible. I claimed that they deserved the opportunity to farm their plots. Mr. Henríquez did not know how to respond, and Dr. Quiñónez intervened, violating the rule established by the judge. He explained that he was not a bad or unfair man, that to avoid problems he always required his land lessees to sign a contract with clear and precise clauses about the rights and obligations of both parties. I asked him to explain which clauses the renters had violated.

The doctor told me there were basically two. First, they arrived to prepare the land using the hacienda's roads, when they could have gone around and come in through other neighboring streets. Secondly, they had not cleared the land. Tree trunks remained that had not been burned or pulled out. As he reported this, he smiled in a way that reminded me of his nickname—the Dark Man—which was a reflection of his sarcastic and hard attitude. His words had no mercy, they did not know human solidarity, and were full of the arrogance characteristic of the large landowner.

Francisco could not take this calmly, and he asked me to show the photos. I let the doctor know that I had visited the rented hacienda plots with Francisco and one of the peasants and that I could see that the tenants had done everything in their power to comply with the contract. I was giving my speech when we heard from the street, on one side of the town hall, multitudinous voices of people who were denouncing the doctor and supporting the campesinos. In the room, there were signs of nervousness. Dr. Quiñónez squirmed in his seat and Mr. Henríquez grew so pale that he looked like a sitting corpse. The judge tried to smile and asked me to continue, reassuring that the matter would not take long.

Given the cynicism of the doctor's statement, I took the opportunity to inject a dose of black humor. I proposed as a solution to the arrival at the hacienda that the doctor rent a helicopter or a small airplane, so that the peasants did not encroach upon his property by passing through it. The campesinos laughed. My solution was stupid, but I meant it to be, to reveal the stupidity of the doctor's accusation. Sometimes one stupid statement must be answered with another to show its absurdity.

The doctor, visibly upset, told the judge, "Father Alas's words demonstrate that he, the student Francisco, and that peasant have trespassed on my lands without my permission, and therefore, I am going to report them and have them charged. But enough of this. Let them enter wherever they please. What I do demand in order to return their plots is that they pull out the tree trunks or set them on fire until they are incinerated."

In my preaching, on various occasions, I have asked the peasants not to burn the land, because of the damage it causes to both the land and the environment. When I heard the doctor's words "burn the tree trunks," I got upset and replied, "Doctor, I propose a better solution"—and I asked the judge's secretary to write down my proposal point by point—"that the trunks that did not catch fire the first time should be left as they are. The devil in hell is going to need those to set you, doctor, on fire because Satan is going to burn you for eternity." As expected, the judge got angry at my proposal for being irreverent of this place and the trial he presides over. He asked me to keep my composure and have some respect. The voices of the protesters increased, as did the nervousness of the judge and the doctor.

The doctor's other son arrived in the room and spoke to his brother, who approached his father and secretly told him something. Father and son got up and made gestures of leaving. The judge intervened and asked them to listen to his verdict: the lands were to be returned to the peasants, but they should not take this as a sign of weakness, but rather one of kindness to them. The doctor, standing, listened to the judge and then left the room in a hurry with his Panama hat in hand, leaning on his cane. His two sons and his "good man" followed him out.

Outside, we met with some four hundred campesino men and women who had come to support their friends' cause. They clapped, crazy with happiness, when they heard the trial's outcome. Don Francisco Villafranco was there, and he seemed to be their leader. Without my knowing it, he and others had organized this demonstration in support of their fellow campesinos. This was my first encounter with the Federation of Salvadoran Christian Campesinos (FECCAS), which would later play one of the most important roles in the peasants' struggles in the country, especially during the civil war years.

Later, at home, I tried to understand the meaning of the trial in which I had participated. It was all new to me, and I felt very happy; I found myself seeking paths in a field unknown to me. I remembered the verse by José Antonio Machado and sung by Juan Manuel Serrat, "*Caminante, se hace camino al caminar.*"[4] I was now quite far from my pastoral ministry in San Salvador city, where I had focused on helping the country's middle and upper classes. I was, for the first time, facing a reality that I needed to live in order to understand it fully and respond to it. This was the new calling I was receiving, from the peasants.

## The Trial's Consequences: Occupation of Suchitoto

I did not have to wait long for the trial's repercussions. The following Tuesday we had a priests' meeting in Domus Mariae, a farm on the capital's outskirts where Monsignor Chávez, Archbishop of San Salvador, had built a clergy meeting center. When I arrived, some of my colleagues approached and showed me the *Prensa Gráfica*, one of the country's newspapers, whose owner is from the Dutriz family of the oligarchy. On the front page and headlined in capital letters as the main news item I read "Suchitoto's Priests Declared Non Gratae by Town Council." There was no relationship between the headline's grandiose size and what happened two days earlier in my town. The news had been exaggerated because we had touched someone with an oligarchic last name, even though Dr. Quiñónez was not all that wealthy.

Father Jorge Miranda, my assistant, and I were accused of being subversives and dangerous, wolves dressed in sheep's clothing, foolish tools of international communism. The reality was that Jorge had nothing to

---

4. "Traveler, the road is made by walking."

do with the matter. It stated that the example we were sowing among the peasant masses could have unpleasant consequences for the whole country, that we were not considering the ramifications of our actions. The article requested that the archbishop move us elsewhere, as if a mere transfer can change a person's mindset. Monsignor Chávez did not mention the matter to me. His years as archbishop had taught him many things about Salvadoran society and reality.

The news spread throughout Suchitoto and its thirty-three cantons. Two or three days later, Don Francisco Villafranco, along with a campesino with the last name Hernández, from Los Palitos valley, came to see me to tell me that the FECCAS leadership had met and decided to summon all the region's campesinos to a rally in our support the following Sunday. This announcement showed me that Suchitoto's peasants already had a good level of organization and were able to summon and mobilize people. I liked what FECCAS proposed; after all, it was their decision. I could not interfere in their affairs; on the contrary, my duty was to encourage them.

On Saturday afternoon Don Toribio Flamenco, an agricultural extension agent very close to the peasant farmers, arrived at my house. He was frightened and alarmed. He asked if I had been outside and I said that I had not. He said, "Well, it would be a good idea for you to go out and see what is happening with your own eyes. There are many national police, rural police, and plainclothes agents on the streets. At least three hundred of them. Suchitoto's population is in an uproar. The peasants' demonstration to be held tomorrow has them worried." I walked around town and confirm what Don Toribio had said—Suchitoto was an occupied city.

Right away, I went to the phone and called Monsignor Chávez. I told him what was happening in the city. He listened to me calmly and told me not to go out, that he would come sleep at my house and officiate at the nine o'clock Sunday morning mass. That afternoon I went to the kitchen and asked Doña Paquita, our household helper, a wonderful person, to prepare a good dinner because the archbishop would be with us that evening and the following day.

Monsignor Chávez arrived, as promised. As my guest, I gave him my room. I felt honored by his presence and, above all, grateful. The pastor's support is essential to building trust within the flock and to continue, with renewed energy, the challenges of the work begun. New paths can be opened without the bishop, but in most cases they will not go far without him. It is a shame there are not many bishops who are also pastors. The majority are mere administrators.

A campesino came to see me and told me that a Red Cross unit had arrived and was parked in front of the National Guard post. He approached it and through the vehicle's window had seen a machine gun mounted inside. He asked me if I was scared. I told him no. He asked me to go myself to confirm his finding. Despite Monsignor Chávez's advice, I left the house and passed the ambulance, but no one said anything to me. I kept on walking, pretending I was going to visit Doña Talita's restaurant.

We ate supper and went to bed. I could not sleep. I thought of tomorrow, of the support the peasants would give us, of the risks they were facing. I tried to craft a picture of the future, but it was closed to me. Experience cannot be read. It is learned, it enters through our own flesh to become a guide in our own path. It is the fruit of time and of accepting life's challenges; in the end, it becomes the synthesis of our good or bad choices.

I celebrated the five o'clock morning mass and on my way home ran into Don Toribio, who told me that some had seen Chele Medrano and Fidel Sánchez Hernández, president of the republic, enter the Guard post. Medrano was one of the country's most infamous murderers, dressed in military uniform and carrying a general's title. At seven, I returned to the house and saw the Monsignor as he came out of my office. He was still adjusting his cassock. I told him that Sánchez and Medrano were in the city. He replied, "Do not worry, I am here. I have been the archbishop of San Salvador for thirty-one years. Those two are full of military bravado. I have seen the rise and fall of eight presidents and look, I am still here. Their luck and their time will be ephemeral, fleeting I will say something during mass." His words were accompanied by a soft smile that inspired confidence. Monsignor was a vigorous man, medium height, and with prominent facial features that came from our indigenous people. He was about seventy years old.

The agents from the National Guard and the police had organized themselves into commands at the four town entrances. The campesinos were trickling in, since it was very early in the morning; they came walking, on horses, by bus, and on trucks. The agents forced them to stop and return to their communities. However, the majority of them, without fear, skirted around the security posts and entered through the cemetery, through backyards, wherever they could.

At nine in the morning, not another soul would have fit inside the church, a beautiful example of colonial architecture that was built last century. Standing and sitting, people were everywhere, and many had stayed outside because there was no room for them inside. Monsignor Chávez entered through the main door. He was happy. The crowd received him with whispers. The children near enough tried to touch his robe, especially the tassels from his red sash with two little balls decorating the fringe. As he advanced, he blessed the crowd, making the sign of the cross with his right hand. It was like a holiday. Father Jorge and I accompanied him. I felt new, like a spoiled child. What a pleasure to have an archbishop like this, committed, without fear.

The celebration of the Eucharist began with an introduction I gave, in which I welcomed the archbishop, especially at this time, and I asked him to bless our town. The choir sang popular religious songs and the parishioners joined in. The important moment of the occasion arrived: the sermon. The archbishop began in the usual way, with the lectionary readings. His sermon seemed very slow; I wanted him to get to the point. He talked about social problems, but made no reference to what was happening outside the church. At the end of mass, before the benediction and with a symbolic smile, he told the crowd: "Go outside, do not go away. Do what you planned to do in the park, everything will be all right." The parishioners understood his words and applauded.

## Campesino Demonstration

We went to the parish house. I invited him to stay a few more hours but he could not because he had other commitments. He asked me to be prudent and to have faith. When I returned to the park, which was just fifty meters in front of the church, a crowd of about four thousand had filled it. I met some deputies of the Christian Democratic Party, among them Mario Zamora, brother of Rubén, who confirmed the presence of agents at the city entrances. They also had to enter through the cemetery so as not to miss the peasants' gathering. One of the organizers was Omar Alas, a law student at the National University and a Suchitoto native, a brave man and friend of many of the peasants present. Omar was with us and was especially moved.

Among the crowd were several plainclothes agents. The deputies recognized them right away because of their behavior, gestures, and above all, their famous Ray-Ban glasses. The speeches followed one after the other.

People applauded and shouted slogans of support. There were two recurring themes during the speeches: the land and their dear priests.

In about an hour I saw Omar, who approached from the town hall. He elbowed his way to the podium. He got up on the platform, asked for the microphone, and told the crowd the following: "Gentlemen, I have just come from city hall, where there is also a meeting of some thirty people of the National Conciliation Party. I saw the mayor, Adrián Lara Guadrón, kneeling at his window. With outstretched arms, he is reciting this prayer: 'Our Father, deliver us from these wolves dressed in sheepskin. Deliver us from these impostor priests who upset the minds of ignorant peasants. Deliver us from communism; may it not reach our doorsteps. Lord, save us, Lord!' Let's all go to city hall to see Don Adrián." Instantly the crowd turned from the park and headed to the town hall, which was a block away. When Don Adrián learned what was happening, he and his chorus of stray politicians left in a stampede. The crowd applauded and shouted; they did not expect to witness such a scene.

Meanwhile, the agents did not know what to do. They had tried to intimidate the peasants with their presence and had not been successful. Although some of them tried to provoke the campesinos to have an excuse to clamp down on them, the peasants maintained the dignity of those who have the right to demonstrate. The archbishop's presence in the city had also restrained the agents and probably made them change their plans.

Two weeks later, an army battalion, along with public security agents, took over the town. The news had spread that the peasants had organized a new rally. Amadeo Acosta, from El Zapote canton, told me on Saturday what they had planned for the next day. It appears the leaders of FECCAS, enthused by the success of the first demonstration, had planned a second one to keep the spirit of struggle alive. Suchitoto's politicians had heard of the plans and had again been in communication with San Salvador. The peasants learned about the troops' arrival in time and did not come into the city. The few who had entered made some small purchases and left immediately. One of them told me a captain stopped him and asked why there had been no demonstration. He replied that no one had planned anything and added, "It was a good thing that you arrived right away, because that way they were not so afraid." Some military officials thought the politicians had deceived them, which greatly annoyed them. Each experience of unity and strength engendered confidence among the peasants. It was a learning process, training for the harder battles of the future.

## Land, Liberation, and Death Squads

Overcrowding and poverty in El Salvador
Photo: Cornell Capa (1972)
International Center of Photography, NY City

Two-story hut in San Salvador
Photo: Cornell Capa (1972)
International Center of Photography, NY City

THE BEGINNING OF A STRUGGLE

## Land Ownership in El Salvador

Dr. Quiñónez was well aware of the unjust practices he employed against peasant farmers that allowed him to grow richer and richer and maintain his powerful status in the city. But anyone who practices injustice creates in him-or herself some inner unrest, in terms of conscience, insecurity, angst, sometimes even deep fear. If someone denounces the unfair practice, calling out the author by name, the perpetrator generally reacts aggressively, making exaggerated counterclaims against his accuser.

This happened in Suchitoto. When injustice is built into the nation's structure, any local pressure has repercussions throughout the country. In fact, oppressors typically possess a collective conscience that prompts them, as a class, to defend and attack, first through the mass media and then with brute force, using "security forces" and the military if necessary. In the end, oppressors are not free. They live chained to their own fears and have to defend themselves in an authoritarian way, or by imposing a dictatorship.

There is no doubt that the country's form of land tenure represents our people's number one problem. It is not a new problem. It goes back to the Spanish conquest, when land was divided into haciendas, a practice that continued in the colonial period and later throughout our time as an "independent" republic. That is the reason why there have been three uprisings since independence from Spain; with each successive revolt, greater numbers have participated and been affected.

The first uprising, in 1833 in the country's southcentral region, was headed by the Pipil Indian Anastasio Aquino, who lived in Santiago Nonualco. The indigenous people could no longer tolerate the living conditions imposed on them by their new post-independence masters in 1821. The creole aristocracy believed the sole purpose of independence was to benefit themselves. Aquino led the revolt against the whites, especially ladinos, those of mixed Spanish and indigenous blood. Aquino began with a massacre of ladinos in Santiago Nonualco. After incorporating thousands of poorly armed indigenous people into his group, he continued the insurrection against the whites in San Vicente, where he was named king of the Nonualcos, wearing the crown of the statue of Saint Joseph. In that city he was defeated, imprisoned, and hanged by the government.

The second revolt took place a hundred years later, in 1932. This time the affected area lay in the country's west. The uprising was directly related to the confiscation of communal and *ejidal* lands carried out by two government decrees in 1880 and 1882, respectively. Ladino hacienda owner

Agustín Farabundo Martí led this rebellion; he rejected the misery imposed upon the people for the mere fact of its inhumanity. This uprising was larger and the ensuing massacre bloodier. Ten- to thirty-thousand people were killed, most of them indigenous. It was, in fact, genocide, perpetrated by General Maximiliano Hernández Martínez.[5]

The last uprising belongs to our era, this time a true civil war encompassing almost the entire country and lasting twelve years, from 1980 to 1992. About eighty thousand people died. As always, the root of this last revolt was inequality of land ownership.

The Salvadoran capitalist has become increasingly more voracious and has accumulated more wealth, allowing him to monopolize more land. Up until 1950, he had confined himself to the agricultural sector, raising coffee, sugarcane, cotton, and cattle. From that decade on he began to diversify his economic base and successfully break into the financial, commercial, and industrial sectors. Until then very few entrepreneurs engaged in international trade; after 1950 more and more ventured into foreign commerce. This modernization program caused capitalists to generate greater wealth, which remains concentrated in their hands. Meanwhile, impoverishment and hunger continued to grow among the people. By the 1970s, only a few eroded hills were left for the cultivation of corn and beans. This unfair situation became the cause of the last civil war we have endured, from 1980 to 1992.

Historically these three uprisings point to a worrisome progression. The 1833 rebellion covered a small area of a few square kilometers and relatively few people died. That of 1932, a hundred years later, became regional, affecting almost the entire western part of the country; it lasted two weeks, and the dead numbered in the thousands, probably thirty thousand. The uprising of the 1980s, scarcely fifty years later, affected the entire country and left about eighty thousand dead. This progression in the deepening of the conflicts leaves us with a chilling question: are these uprisings finished, or will there be others ten to twenty years from now? The causes have been somewhat alleviated, but not yet eliminated fully. Therefore, under current conditions no one can assure us a better future.

In 1976, Father P. Ignacio Ellacuría, SJ,[6] wrote the following:

---

5. A thorough discussion of whether the 1932–33 repression constituted genocide may be found in Gould and Lauria-Santiago, *To Rise in Darkness*, 219–221.

6. Father Ellacuria was among those assassinated in a vicious attack at the Universidad de Centroamerica on November 16, 1989.

> The capitalists should not forget that, even from their own viewpoints, the country's current social situation is unsustainable, and even more so that of the countryside and peasants. If property is necessary for liberty, the majority of Salvadoran peasants lack this indispensable condition of liberty. If property is the fruit of work, and is based in it, we must conclude that the secular labor of Salvadoran peasants is not humane work, because it should have produced for them property they do not have. Consequently, to go against the current form of ownership would only be to go against the public interest, and it will only go against social peace because of a minority, since the majority would not lose stability by acquiring what they do not now have; if uncontrolled forces are awakened, it will be at the instigation of those who do not want to see the common good.[7]

In our country, before the war, the land issue allowed the development of a dynamic that was the trigger for a range of values, problems, struggles, and aspirations. It was because of the land that rural men and women joined the Farabundo Martí National Liberation Front (FMLN). That explains why 90 percent of the guerilla forces were of peasant origin. The war that began in 1980 and ended twelve years later, at the cost of eighty thousand deaths and the destruction of much of the country's infrastructure, never originated in an East-West confrontation, as Reagan presented it to an ignorant or callous US Congress. The war was due to the hunger and nudity our people suffer because of the land monopoly and its dedication to export crops. Reagan, idol of many US-Americans, will always be remembered in Central America as a monster of the same cut as Hitler, who paid mercenaries in Nicaragua and colonels in El Salvador to kill innocent children, women, and elderly in our streets and forests, and our best young people, in the name of liberty and the interests of the "US dollar."

The incident at the Aguas Calientes Hacienda and its repercussions, which we will shortly go into, demand of us a critical and ethical judgment, and make us ask whether a ministry that does not take into account land tenure makes any sense. This unjust ownership is, at its base, structural sin, which permanently creates a violent situation. A ministry that looks heavenward must still be rooted in the soil, and in El Salvador the soil does not belong to everyone. The God of Salvation cannot be in contradiction with the God of Creation; they are one and the same, and the land is God's creation for us. The "us" is all of us, not just a handful of individuals.

7. Ignacio Ellacuría, "A sus órdenes, mi capital," 649–656.

*Chapter 2*

# Theological Sources of the Suchitoto Ministry

This chapter is important for explaining the theological sources from which the religious and social endeavors in Suchitoto flowed. All ministries are guided by an underlying theology. Without the theology that inspired us, the events described in the following chapters would be mere anecdotes, however interesting they might be.

### The Second Vatican Council and Being Church

One cannot explain the maturing of adult faith and commitment to the poor of El Salvador and elsewhere without taking into account the espousal of Vatican II's message. The Vatican II became the cornerstone upon which a new way of being church was built. Archbishop Luis Chávez y González was the one who placed this cornerstone that was later inherited by the martyred archbishop Óscar Romero. The Second Vatican Council was a revelation for him and for us all.

The Council was felt in the archdiocese from the moment it began on October 11, 1962. That day we held a procession in the capital that I had organized with seminarians; more than ten thousand people from all walks of life participated in it. We organized ourselves into one hundred groups of one hundred individuals apiece, each with a leader in front who read Bible verses for all to meditate upon. Everyone carried a candle, creating a river of light. The procession began at the Divine Savior of the World statue and ended at Libertad Plaza, a four-kilometer walk. From then on, the Council was of continual interest to everyone. As each document was approved and published, multiple working groups of clergy and parishioners analyzed it under Monsignor Chávez's direct leadership.

Vatican II coincided with the first years of the Cuban Revolution, which proved the possibility of liberation from dictatorships like that of Batista and his ally from the north, the United States. It also coincided with the appearance of dependency theory, which focused on demonstrating the root causes of the growing poverty in Latin America and the Third World in general. The countries on the periphery could free themselves from the existing unjust situation if they could break the chains of inhumane capitalism that bound them like new slaves.

The final council document approved in 1965, the Pastoral Constitution of the Church in the Modern World, had a singular impact. Its very preamble became the subject of much commentary. It constituted good news. In it, the church says:

> The joys and the hopes, the grief, and the anxieties of the people of this age, especially those who are poor or in any way afflicted, these are the joys and hopes, the grief and anxieties of the followers of Christ. Indeed, nothing genuinely human fails to raise an echo in their hearts. For theirs is a community composed of men and women. United in Christ, they are led by the Holy Spirit in their journey to the Kingdom of their Father and they have welcomed the news of salvation which is meant for every individual. That is why this community realizes that it is truly linked with humankind and its history by the deepest of bonds.[1]

This insertion of the church into the world and history, together with the new yet very old—albeit forgotten—theology of its constitution, sows hope in the hearts of committed laypeople, and later of the poor. The concept of people and people of God reappears from its biblical roots. Thus collapses the pyramid of the First Vatican Council, convened from 1869 to 1870, which had placed the pope and the hierarchy of bishops at the peak. They are redefined as servants of the community and part of it.

## The Liturgy

The Council's other major stride came in the liturgy. As the Benedictine monk Lambert Beauduin wrote for the closing ceremony of the Congress of Liturgy held in 1932 in Liège, Belgium, the liturgy needed to be

---

1. Pope Paul VI, *Gaudium et Spes*, paragraph 1.

"democratized," and first, de-Latinized. When people hear Bible readings in their own language, they discover their history and faith heritage, which had been hidden, cloaked in a dead language, unseen, an inheritance of the insiders, thus becoming another vestige of power and cultural oppression.

Chencho Alas preaching in the Santa Lucia church
Photo: Cornell Capa (1972)
International Center of Photography, NY City

## The Bible

From hearing Bible readings in mass, people take the next logical step of reading Scripture at home or in groups; in this way Latin America's Christian Base Communities began.

These communities gather around the Bible, to read life in a context of faith-proclamation-message. They had had enough of faith as doctrine.

Faith as doctrine is dead. It presumes knowledge, which may or may not be linked to the facts. Faith as a message proclaimed is good news. Intrinsic to the message is the need to transform reality. The message analyzes the situation, and if it is found unacceptable, harmful, destructive, or oppressive, it demands change: both inner conversion and changes to the external structures.

When people begin to read the Bible on their own, they experience a gradual change in the handed-down mindset, a mindset full of abstract statements, with an affirmation like "I believe in the all-powerful God" suggestive of a far-off God, not Jesus's father, our parent. Some describe this mentality as Greek, because it thrives on ideas and is idealistic. It differs from the Hebrew and Aramaic mind, which is concrete, historical. An example is the following: Aristotle ponders whether God is creator; the Israelite, on the other hand, simply affirms that God created all things. For the latter, there is no question: creative facts are on display. Moving from the Greek to Hebraic mindset is essential, since theology, and especially ministry, should be concerned with the historical realities of yesterday and today, with a view to the utopian and eschatological, always in search of new paradigms.

## The Second Conference of Latin American Bishops (Medellín)

Another important wellspring of pastoral inspiration is Medellín, as we refer to the Second Conference of Latin American Bishops, held in that Colombian city in August 1968. In content and impact, it divides the history of the Latin American church in two, a *before* and an *after* Medellín. Besides the bishops, this conference was attended by the continent's most intellectually committed and experienced men and women—not only theologians, biblical scholars, and ministers, but also sociologists, historians, anthropologists, and practitioners of other sciences related to Christian work.

Latin American bishops had attended Vatican II like silent sheep guided by European shepherds. Some of them went to Rome, but Rome did not come to them; they remained in the Vatican cafeteria. Others, yes, understood Pope John XXIII's symbolic gesture of opening his window when he announced the Council as a sign of a new breeze he wanted for his church. Because of this, these bishops desired a council of their own. With this goal they met in Medellín, where they became the actors. Their intent was to apply the teachings of Vatican II to Latin America, and in this they succeeded. They became the subjects of their own reflection, responsible for their own destiny and the destiny of the many entrusted to their care.

The preparation for Medellín lasted two intense years, during which parishes and dioceses discussed the preparatory document. Those comments were presented to the assembly of bishops. The dominant themes of the discussions, and later in the officially approved conclusions, were the following:

- Institutionalized injustice and the need for justice for the poor;
- Peace as a response to the state of structural violence;
- The unity of history and the political dimension of faith;
- Participation of laypeople in building the church via their own historical insertion into the world.

## The Institutes of the Latin American Episcopal Conference

Along with the above sources, we should mention the role played by the institutes of social science, liturgy, and pastoral ministry of the Latin American Episcopal Conference that operated for several years in Chile, Colombia, and Ecuador. Many of the experts who advised the bishops in Medellín were professors in these centers of study, analysis, and discussion. In 1968, I studied in the Latin American Pastoral Institute (IPLA), in Quito, Ecuador, where I served as the first student president.

IPLA was entrusted with working on the draft on pastoral work. The professors who worked with us at IPLA have been some of the most important contributors to liberation theology: Enrique Düssel, the two Segundos, José Comblin, and others. It is a pity that the bishops' blindness, due to their fear of a sure loss of alliance with established power, led them to close these centers. Ignorance is fear's best motivator; unfortunately, many bishops are ignorant.

Elías Acosta, later martyred, distributes Holy Communion
Photo: Cornell Capa (1972)
International Center of Photography, NY City

## Liberation Theology

In the theological field, the largest contribution to the ministry in Latin America—and of course in Suchitoto—comes from liberation theology. The theology in which the majority of pastors have been educated is doctrinal; it has been reduced to rational knowledge. It is not evangelical, it does not represent the good news of a reality that must be transformed. It is a theology seeded in dichotomies: secular history and sacred history, the human and the divine, matter and spirit, body and soul, the faithful and the hierarchy, natural and supernatural, and so forth.

Characteristic of these dichotomies is the contradiction implicit in each, or at least in presenting them as different realities. Vatican II erases these conceptions and presents us with a single story with a single calling when it affirms, "Christ died for all, and the ultimate calling of each person is in fact one, that is, the divine." This is because "by his incarnation the son of God has united himself in some way with every person."[2]

From this reality that gives unity to the life of each man and woman in Jesus, Christians acquire the right to do theology through baptism and confirmation. Every Christian is a theologian. If one's life is oppressed, one's theological task will be to seek and fight for liberation. The demands of real life, considering its divine calling, requires everyone to do theology according to the result to be achieved. In Latin America the liberation of the poor is not a preferred option, but an obligation of our faith.

The contents of liberation theology can be easily reduced to two central points: the historical Jesus and the poor. God's people are all of us who are baptized; there is no exclusion of race, social position, and so on. However, within God's people there are many, a majority, who need liberation from institutionalized injustice, from the structures of sin, so that they may experience peace and love in their lives. That majority are the poor. Moreover, they must be the center of their own liberation. Jesus has been presented in different ways, under different conceptions, often as the result of reflections that are not always Christians. There is, however, only one way to get close to him, that of the Gospels, Jesus-in-history, because we are concerned with reality, not ideas, as elegant and beautiful as the latter may be.

Naturally, the topic of Jesus generates many subthemes, as does the issue of the poor. This will be the purpose of the following paragraphs. We must remember that theology is second here; it is reflection. What is primary is the person of Jesus, that is, the poor themselves, who are of his flesh. This reflection is not intended to remain a mere reflection; instead, it returns to its source as a message, a transforming force of historical reality whenever that reality should be changed.

For our purposes, we distinguish between two notions of poverty: material poverty as an evil crying out to heaven and spiritual poverty, or disposition to the Lord's will. Regarding the first: we define poverty as the lack of possessions basic to human dignity. The possessions can be of a material or spiritual nature. Poverty of a material nature includes lack of food, clothing, shelter, health, and/or the means of production. Material poverty of a spiritual nature may involve lack of education, unemployment, exploitation in work, lack of incentives to live, and/or lack of others' solidarity with us and ours with others. *The symbol of material poverty is death.*

---

2. Ibid, paragraph 22.

On the other hand, the second poverty, spiritual poverty, is a spiritual gift that allows us to put all our trust in God. Through our openness to the Spirit we have the certainty that God is with us, and that God has a plan we should fulfill for our lives. That plan may be one of sacrifice and pain, as in the case of Jesus and Mary, but it is a plan that ennobles us and is of service to others, to our neighbors. It is inspired by solidarity. This spiritual gift is not in contradiction with the possession of material goods, if those goods contribute to the fulfillment of God's plan. After all, "The symbol of spiritual poverty is life and life in abundance."[3]

## Increased Poverty in the Last Thirty Years

Poverty in recent years is rooted in Central America. It has been growing, too often reaching the level of misery. The amelioration of poverty has seriously regressed, bringing about violence.

From 1952 to 1968, Central American countries sustained annual growth rates of 5 percent. The growth was due in part to the boom in the world economy, to the flow of financial assistance and investment, and to policies favorable to agricultural diversification, marketing, and local industrialization. During that period, per capita income doubled and the region's countries invested in multiple public works and experienced relative peace. It was also the era of the Alliance for Progress, which tried to change our people's way of life while maintaining the region's dependency on the North. It was a mere modernization of the system and adoption of new forms, without changes in the sociopolitical or economic structures. Such substantive changes can only be the result of a revolution, carried out, of course, by those who suffer the existing oppression.

In fact, the modernization injected into the region was but the introduction of more aggressive forms of agro-exportation. These suffer, however, from a permanent structural weakness. Prices of coffee, sugar, and cotton do not depend upon domestic markets. Any change in price, favorable or unfavorable, deeply affects earnings from these commodities.

The agro-export model, with its "Green Revolution" technology, is voracious; it needs more land dedicated to export products. This means that the landless people increase rapidly, almost in geometric progression. Greater wealth also means greater poverty. If to this we add El Salvador's legacy of land distribution from the late nineteenth century, with the

3. John 10:10.

famous decrees that abolished communal and *ejidal* lands, in 1880 and 1882 respectively, the problem naturally gets bigger.

In the late 1950s some of the region's planners, with the support of the Economic Commission for Latin America (ECLA), acknowledged the profound weaknesses of the agro-export model and proposed a new import-substitution program. It aimed to correct the system with protective tariffs and by regionalizing industrial production, manufacturing, and product marketing. Even with such policies, by the early 1970s the consequences of agro-export policies began to be felt. The entire region started to import food, after having been self-sufficient in food production. In addition, with the indiscriminate use of chemicals to obtain the greatest productivity, the land gradually became contaminated, which has generated environmental problems of serious concern such as health issues, soil depletion, and water and air poisoning.

One of the countries that took most advantage of the two models was El Salvador. Bear in mind that El Salvador's private sector is very aggressive in the financial and economic fields, and its people are extremely hardworking. This is in stark contrast to neighboring Honduras, characterized as one of the region's poorest countries. The adoption of the import-substitution model came to favor Salvadoran businesses and, as a result, deepened the developmental imbalance of the two countries. El Salvador virtually became a colonizer of its neighbor.

This was the cause of the 1969 war between the two countries, which lasted barely one hundred hours. This brevity was thanks to the intervention of the Organization of American States (OAS) and the fact that both armies lacked the means for further conflict. The war had the universal support of each country's populace, its organizations and political parties, including the communists. It was a demonstration of extreme *machismo*. Very few of us criticized it openly. I did so, but fearfully. In a sermon in Aguacayo, I called it the "War of the Beggars"; this reached the government's ears, causing distaste, naturally, among the military.

The war's consequences were disastrous for the region and especially for its people. It marked the end of the Central American Economic Market, which had produced a degree of regional integration. For example, trade among the five countries grew from 4 to 35 percent between 1960 and 1969. This growth was not equally distributed among Central Americans; on the contrary, it came to favor the existing elites, who became partners of foreign capital. Moreover, as new development required the importing of raw materials and machinery from abroad, costs of local products skyrocketed and could not compete in quality or price with the imported goods. All of this resulted in the failure of the import-substitution model throughout Central America.

To all this must be added the additional consequence that for several years Honduras, in reprisal for the war, closed the Pan-American Highway linking El Salvador with Nicaragua and Costa Rica. This was another reason for the further impoverishment of the Salvadoran people.

Lastly, many Salvadoran families who had immigrated to Honduras returned to El Salvador. These families, numbering about ten thousand people in all, began to put more pressure on the peasants' demand for land, which helped form a more critical awareness of the need for agrarian reform. The landed oligarchy historically opposed such reform using all means at their disposal, including genocide, as they proved in 1932 with the killing of some thirty thousand persons, the majority of them indigenous people.

In short, from 1950 to 1970 El Salvador achieved sustained economic growth through the application of two complementary models: agro-exportation and import-substitution. These two models contain within them the seeds of their own destruction. Meanwhile, the growth did not benefit the vast majority of Salvadorans. On the contrary, while they witnessed growing wealth and luxury for the few, they sunk deeper into poverty and oppression. At the same time, this situation brought about new awareness that generated responses which changed the face of the country. Reflecting upon these responses, analyzing them in the light of faith in Jesus, is the very object of theology; such work constitutes theological reflection.

In addition to theology, in Suchitoto's case, which is what concerns me, I also used cultural anthropology as an auxiliary science. I do not think good pastoral work can be done without taking into account people's values, attitudes, and lifestyles. Jesus's incarnation occurred within a culture, that of the Jewish people. The incarnation of Jesus's message today should take place within each and every one of the planet's cultures.

## Chapter 3

# A Demonstration in San Salvador
## *The La Asunción Hacienda*

### Eviction Orders

NEWS OF THE SAN Juan canton campesinos' victory in the Suchitoto magistrate's court spread like wildfire through the neighboring cantons and even reached many other parts of the country. This positive result encouraged the region's Celebrants of the Word, FECCAS members, and non-organized peasants to face new struggles and new problems, one of which involved the La Asunción hacienda.

The importance of this second case rests in the fact that for the first time campesinos confronted a corporation, *Parcelaciones Rurales para el Desarollo* (Rural Subdivisions Development), located in San Salvador, whereas in the first they dealt with an individual, Dr. Quiñónez.

La Asunción hacienda dates back to colonial times. It is located between Suchitoto and La Toma de Aguilares, at the foot of Guazapa Hill and not far from the Lempa River, the country's main source of water and electricity. Apparently, one of La Asunción's previous owners was the priest Matias Delgado, El Salvador's father of independence in 1821. The current tenant farmers' great-great-grandparents must surely have known this famous figure of El Salvador's history. Its most recent owner did not know how to manage the hacienda and decided to sell it to Parcelaciones Rurales para el Desarollo, a newly established corporation that was growing by leaps and bounds. The president of the company was Roberto Hill, coffee grower and financier of British descent.

A group of peasants affiliated with FECCAS came to visit me because some of their friends had received eviction notices. If they did not leave on good terms, they would instead be forced out by the National Guard. They were permitted to buy the plots on which they lived, but the asking prices were prohibitive. One of them had said, "Not even if I sold all my chickens, my hogs, my children and my wife could I pay Parcelaciones for a piece of that land." In fact, prices per *manzana*[1] had been set very high. A manzana of poor land cost six hundred *colones*; of good land, one thousand or more; and of irrigated land, up to three thousand. At that time, one US dollar exchanged for 2.50 Salvadoran colones. These prices were well above what a poor tenant farmer could afford. I asked them what they had planned as a way to demand their right to live on land on which they and generations before them were born, land passed from father to son, land they had seen flourish, produce, and now were supposed to abandon. After all, they had no other place to go.

The tenant farmer is dependent on the landowner, but he receives some benefits for the work he does on the land. He is part slave, part free. Until recently, no value was put on the tenant farmer's labor in the national economy. The hacienda had its own store in which tenant farmers bought everything they needed: sugar, coffee, lard, beans, rice, and other foodstuffs, even clothing and medicine. They paid for these goods using tokens redeemable only on the landowner's property. The tenant farmer was always in debt, and therefore could not leave the place where he lived. If he did, he could easily fall into the hands of the National Guard, the rural security force founded in 1912 with the help of the famous Spanish Guard. In the beginning, the Guards' tasks were to watch over rural property, arrest "vagabonds"—even though they might be people moving around to look for work—and to maintain order in the countryside. Over time, this security force became one of the most repressive in the country's history, especially under the leadership of General Medrano from the early 1970s until its abolition as part of the negotiated 1992 Peace Accords. There were also haciendas with their own private guards and jails. Such was the case with the country's largest estate, the Nancuchiname Hacienda, owned by the Dueñas family.

---

1. A "manzana" is a unit of land equivalent to approximately 1.75 acres.

The great majority of haciendas had no schools, since landowners saw no need for peasants to have such luxuries. I remember a story my friend Father Abad, a descendant of cattle ranchers in Medellín, Colombia, told me. Abad tended to the "spiritual" needs of many of San Salvador's wealthy families. On Sundays he would go to their haciendas, sometimes celebrating mass with the peasants living there. On one such occasion, he asked the peasants if the children had a school, and the parishioners said no, because the owner had no interest in having them learn to read and write. He asked if they would like to have a school and naturally they all said yes. At lunchtime, while eating with his friends in the manor house, the heart of the estate, Abad naively told them what had happened in the service, about his conversation with the parishioners. The owner, his friend, furious with rage, his face red, stood up and yelled, "Now why did you go and talk to those idiots about school! Do you not see that if they learn to read, they will get all uppity and cause me problems! For a long time I have managed to keep them uninterested in such things and now you come along! Father, we are good friends but that no longer matters; I want you to leave this house right now. I do not want communist priests as family friends." Abad could do nothing but say goodbye to the owner's wife and children and leave, never to return.

Coffee pickers sleep in the streets of Santa Tecla (1972)
Photo: Cornell Capa (1972)
International Center of Photography, NY City

## Demonstration in Front of the Hacienda

I asked the campesinos what they planned to do. They told me they thought it would be good to hold a demonstration in front of the hacienda's main gate, with two hundred or more people in attendance. They had the support of FECCAS, which was well organized in that whole region. I accepted their proposal and we set the date. We needed time to call the people together, so we gave ourselves two weeks. It was 1969, in the middle of the year, which meant we had to take rainy season into account. A storm could spoil it all. We decided on eleven in the morning, to allow time for those campesinos who lived far away, several hours' walk from the hacienda. Ninety-nine percent of them had no means of transportation, either their own or someone else's.

The day arrived and I was there. About one hundred fifty people had gathered, most of them campesinos. Two National Assembly representatives for Suchitoto district also came out, one of them with the last name Escobar. We did not know how they had heard about our rally. As usual, the speeches started. The FECCAS leaders lashed out at the voracious land appetites of those who do not need more property. They each ended their speeches with the slogan, "Land for those who work it." The tenant farmers spoke of their poverty and the impossibility of buying the plots on which they lived. Some women wept and lifted children in their arms, to show they were especially worried about their children. Ultimately in such situations, it is children and women who suffer the most.

They asked me to intercede and in my speech I made clear the need for agrarian reform that would benefit campesinos. I let the assembled know that Rural Subdivisions Development is indeed carrying out land reform, but for the benefit of urban professionals and businessmen, who could afford plots of fifty manzanas or more. It was a liberal reform, made by a well-known private company for the benefit of that company's members. The idea behind such a reform, I had heard, came from Francisco de Sola, who believed subdividing the land would multiply the number of people owning land and thus avoid a social explosion. But for Roberto Hill, Miguel Salaverría, and their cronies, de Sola's proposal was nothing more than a brilliant idea that would allow them to get richer and richer.

Representative Escobar asked for the floor and he was given it. He let the demonstrators know that campesinos could not fully analyze the situation for lack of data and knowledge. For example, in the region to be subdivided, there would be more property owners with the means to cultivate the land. That would translate into increased demand for labor, whether full time or for longer periods of seasonal work. After all, the land had been idle and would be put into production. The campesinos shook their heads no. They had not been told anything new. Their fate, to work for one boss or another, would always be the same, that of semi-enslaved tenant farmers, underpaid day laborers, or as third- or fourth-class workers.

The rally ended and I asked the leaders to come to my house to critique the event. We needed to evaluate it. While I was speaking with them, the district assemblyman signaled that he needed to talk with me. I followed him to one side, and he confidentially proposed the following: "Look, we know you want to start an agricultural school for the campesinos, that you have been talking about it. I am authorized to tell you that Parcelaciones is willing to give you the manor house and fifty manzanas surrounding it for that purpose. It is good land and the house is a colonial jewel. You should go look at it inside." I reply that I am familiar with it, and grateful to him, but that in these circumstances I cannot accept his generous and tempting offer. Inside I was telling myself, what a shame I cannot accept, but I should not; I would betray the campesinos if I accepted. It certainly would have been a beautiful center for an agricultural school for campesinos. The manor house is a huge old home built in colonial times, probably in the early seventeenth century, with walls about a meter thick and hand-carved columns. Its beams are of a valuable wood, resistant to woodworm, and the roof is of giant tiles. A stone wall surrounds it and the courtyards are carpeted in river gravel, small and fine. A school there would have been a luxury, a dream come true.

In the afternoon I met with the FECCAS leaders. Their critique centered on the small number of rally participants. I asked them if they thought the event would have any effect on public opinion, if it would put some pressure on Parcelaciones Rurales. They said they doubted it. More likely, Parcelaciones' directors considered it a gathering of a few powerless small fry and would continue to evict the tenant farmers.

## Demonstration in the Capital

We asked ourselves what more we could do. Someone proposed a march in the capital, with banners and posters. I thought it was an excellent idea, but we would have to throw all our effort into it. We would have to organize committees and especially work on publicity. The enthusiasm spread. I told them that the Celebrants of the Word—campesino leaders of the ministry in the cantons—would announce the demonstration in each community's religious services and they would be able to motivate people. We gave ourselves two weeks. We could not wait any longer than that because National Guardsmen had already thrown some of the tenant farmers out of their shacks and into the street with their meager belongings.

Those two weeks were ones of feverish activity. I went from canton to canton inviting the campesinos; the Celebrants of the Word and FECCAS leaders did the same. Our aim was a mass demonstration in San Salvador that would represent the campesinos' interests.

We met after a week to review our level of preparation. In the meeting it occurred to me that it would be good to have the presence of campesinos from other regions of the country. However, it was already too late to invite them and we lacked a quick means of mobilization. Given this, I proposed that we paint banners and placards with the names of other towns and cities that read: "Campesinos of Usulután," "Campesinos of Cojutepeque," "Campesinos of Santa Ana," and so forth, pretending to have national representation. Everyone liked the idea. After all, El Salvador is small; they were familiar with many of the places and would be able to say something about them if asked about them during the demonstration.

It was Tuesday. I got up at four in the morning. Many of the campesinos had come to sleep at the rectory. We had a cup of coffee with sweet rolls and left, everyone on their own, for San Salvador. We would rendezvous in front of *La Constancia*, the beer factory, a monopoly of the Meza Ayau, Sol, Quiñonéz, Murray, and other families, located on the famous Avenida at the capital's east entrance.

When I arrived with my group of campesinos, there were already several hundred forming lines in a highly disciplined manner. I was greatly satisfied when I saw many of the signs and banners with the names of the country's different departments. For those unaware of the strategy, the impression was that of a national demonstration, although, truth be told, the campesinos were only from Suchitoto and Aguilares, the neighboring parish. We would have had more people if the Jesuits had already been in Aguilares. They arrived in that parish three years later. Suchitoto parish was actually the first to take on such adventures and was therefore isolated in the region. In the neighboring parishes, such as Guayabal, San Bartolomé Perulapía, San Francisco Chalatenango, and Aguilares, the parish priests maintained a very conservative attitude, some opposed to, or simply with no interest in, involvement in social issues.

We began the march to the National Palace, located in the city center, next to the cathedral under construction. The palace was constructed in the early twentieth century, of heavy architecture and was very neglected. It lacked the elegance of Guatemala's palaces. This is the meeting place of the legislative assembly, to which we were going to deliver petitions in favor of the tenant farmers of the La Asunción Hacienda and in the general interests of the country's campesinos.

Child going to pick coffee
Photo: Cornell Capa (1972)
International Center of Photography, NY City

## The Clergy's Reaction to the Demonstration

That day the clergy had their monthly meeting in Domus Mariae. On the first Tuesday of each month, the clergy of the Archdiocese of San Salvador met to study issues relating to pastoral work. I stayed with the campesinos for a good while, and then I went to Domus Mariae. I wanted to tell the clergy about the demonstration going on in San Salvador's streets and speak out against the land tenure situation. Knowing that many of the campesinos lacked money to buy food and pay for the return trip to their cantons, I also wanted to take up a collection among the clergy to defray those expenses.

I arrived at Domus Mariae and went right into the room in which the clergy were meeting. I had a lot of trust in Monsignor Chávez, which allowed me to ask for the floor right away. He likely saw my worried countenance, for he allowed me to speak, interrupting the discussion underway.

I quickly told them about what was happening to the La Asunción Hacienda's tenant farmers and about how my parish's campesinos decided to hold a protest rally in San Salvador, which was taking place at that very minute. Judging by some of my colleagues' facial expressions, I understood that not all were pleased with the matter; they shifted in their seats and whispered among themselves. Father Flores, my predecessor in Suchitoto, murmured something in the ear of Toño Rivas, one of the archdiocese's most aggressively conservative priests. Most of the younger priests, by contrast, showed signs of joy, of real support for the campesinos' action.

What I least expected, a tremendous argument, ensued, mediated by the archbishop's kindness and patience. Alfonso Navarro and Tilo Sánchez, recently ordained priests, spoke up in enthusiastic support for me. Others agreed that there was a problem with land grabbing on the part of a few landowners, but they believed the clergy should not get involved in "those things," as it is neither their responsibility nor their role. Some, such as a Somascan[2] priest at the Church of our Lady of Guadalupe, located among wealthy neighborhoods, furiously attacked me and hastily read paragraphs from a papal encyclical to support his arguments. The trouble was that the reference to the Vatican's document had little to do with the subject we were discussing. He finished by accusing me of being a communist and an atheist.

I was tired. I had been working long hours for many days and my fuse was short. I replied in the only way it seems the priest would understand me, directly. I said to him, "Imagine, Father, that we priests can marry, there is no church law against it, and that you are not careful and you have twelve children, one after the other, all young, a perfect *marimba* of them." Tilo was nearby and I heard him say, "Poor woman!" I continued "Imagine now that all these children ask for food and clothing, that one of them gets sick, your wife is unwell, and you live in a shack, with no job and no land. What would you do? Stand there with your arms crossed? Get on your knees and simply pray to God?" Monsignor Chávez interrupted me. I had raised my voice; I indeed have a strong voice that I do not control well, and I had lost my composure. Monsignor said, "We understand these things, but we need to get back to our agenda."

2. The Somascans are an order of Catholic priests.

Monsignor Jorge Castro Peña, who thought highly of me, asked to speak to wrap up the discussion. He suggested that each of them, according to his principles and generosity, contribute, if he could, a few colones for the campesinos. He added that no one is obligated to give if not in agreement with what I was doing. Then he extended his hand to give me a generous donation, to set an example. My young colleagues passed a basket and we collected about three hundred colones. I received the offering gladly, then I thanked them and said goodbye. I returned to where I should have been, alongside the campesinos who were defending their rights.

## The Legislative Assembly Lowers the Land Prices

A few days later, thanks to some assemblymen of the Christian Democratic Party, especially Mario Zamora, a decree was published mandating that Parcelaciones Rurales para el Desarollo lower the price of a manzana of land to two hundred fifty colones for the tenant farmers of the La Asunción Hacienda. Victory had been achieved, after the assemblymen held a few meetings with Parcelaciones's directors in the legislative chamber.

The victory should not be lost to memory; it should undergo an evaluation. That was what we did. In a meeting of community leaders, we critiqued the demonstration and its results. We concluded that taking to the streets to proclaim campesinos' rights depends upon their being organized in every canton, in every community, and upon their prompt response, at the right time, to the oppressors' acts of injustice.

That same week a campesino came to thank me for my participation in the San Salvador demonstration. Filled with satisfaction, he said, "This is good, we are winning!" In other words, trust was taking root in the campesino's heart. Trust is a value that for centuries the system of oppression has tried to strip from the consciousness of the weakest. They cannot trust, not even in themselves, much less in others. They live in distrust as a defense, because they have no democracy, which represents a civilized way of living in community and the best manifestation of an organized people.

Certainly, out of the land problem and the just solutions being sought for it, a set of cultural values was being reborn, values that had disappeared due to the Spanish conquest, colonialism, and the brutal emergence of peripheral capitalism during our country's era of independence. About this I will say more later.

*Chapter 4*

# Forging Community Leaders
## The Christian Base Communities

### Background

IN THIS AND THE next chapter I will describe the beginnings of the organizational processes in Suchitoto related to evangelization and their impact in social work. My focus will be how these related to land tenure and the beginning of a politicization of the campesinos. The actors in these processes were, first, the campesinos themselves, and, second, the team of priests who served the communities.

My academic background and work in the fields of evangelization and social development necessarily determined the focus of my service in Suchitoto. After studying philosophy at the San José de la Montaña Seminary in San Salvador, I went to Sherbrooke, Canada, where I began to study theology. During the two years I studied in that country, what impacted me most was Bishop Georges Cabana's celebration of the liturgy in the cathedral. From Bishop Cabana, who had a doctorate in the subject, my love of the liturgy was born. I consider the liturgy not only an instrument to celebrate our thanks to God, but also as a vehicle that can nourish substantial change in one's vision of the world and of one's neighbors. I continued my studies in the Pontifical Gregorian University in Rome and was ordained a priest in the period of the immortal Pope John XXIII. I did my theology graduation thesis on man in Nietzsche and Dostoyevsky. The subject of the human (he and she) has been one of the most important in my life's work. After Rome, I went to Brussels to study catechism at the Lumen Vitae International Institute.

Upon returning to El Salvador in 1960, I worked for a few months in Mejicanos and then I started cursillos de Cristiandad with Toño Punyed, a twenty-two-year-old Spaniard. Later I founded *Jornadas de Vida Cristiana* for university students. In each case I poured all my passion and hope into the work to achieve the best results.

Before coming to Suchitoto I studied in Quito in 1968, at the Latin American Pastoral Institute. The experience in Quito was the most enriching of my student life due to the quality of the visiting professors who came to speak with us. It was in Quito where I became familiar with the concept of Christian Base Communities.

In Suchitoto, Fathers Tilo Sánchez and Jorge Miranda worked hand in hand with me for a few months. In 1970 my brother Higinio joined us; he had studied theology in Guatemala and pedagogy in San Salvador and done pastoral work in Quito. That year, Father Bernardo Boulang, a Frenchman, visited us. A specialist in pastoral ministry with rural youth, Father Boulang became enthusiastic about our work and decided to join our team. And lastly Father Jesús Ángel Bengoechea, SJ, joined us in 1971 for about a year; he was very interested in learning about rural ministry. Prior to my decision to remain working in Suchitoto, something providential happened that created, I would say, the circumstances that gave rise to all my pastoral contribution to the region. The providential incident, to which I later allude, was attending to a dying man that led me into deep reflection.

In 1968, the district of Suchitoto—an indigenous word meaning "bird on a flower"—was inhabited by about forty-five thousand people, 30 percent of whom lived in the city and 70 percent in the thirty-three cantons spread over an area of 265 square kilometers.

Suchitoto is situated between the Lempa River and the famous Guazapa Hill. According to colonial custom, a plaza is located in the town's center; the church, built in the last century, is on one side of the plaza. The Santa Lucía Church is one of the country's most beautiful. Cigar-making is the city's cultural inheritance. Everywhere, in large houses and small, there are women hanging tobacco leaves to dry, chopping the dried leaves, or rolling the tobacco into larger pieces to make cigars. Suchitoto, once known for growing and processing indigo, has never experienced either extreme poverty or extreme wealth. At one time, at the beginning of the twentieth century, it was the home of relatively rich families who later moved to San

Salvador. Two presidents and various illustrious figures in the country's life have come from this area.

A characteristic of the town has been its political rebelliousness and awakened political spirit. Some of the older men still tell of their participation in Dr. Arturo Romero's party, how they were jailed during the pro-democracy riots in 1944, and harassed for their political affiliation. That was the case, for instance, with Don Eduardo Flamenco. Every day, very early, the guards took him from his cell and threatened to shoot him by firing squad.

When I arrived in Suchitoto in December 1968, there were only two large estates in the area: the Colima Hacienda, property of the three Orellana brothers, who had a mill to grind sugarcane; and the seven sugarcane plantations of the Queen Mother of Holland, also with its own mill, called San Francisco, administered by Kurt Nottebohn, a German. There were other smaller properties, owned by the Gallardos of Santa Tecla, the Paradas, the Quiñonéz family, and others from Suchitoto. These were properties of up to three thousand five hundred manzanas in size. The rest of the population owned small farms or were landless agricultural workers. Medium-sized properties were scarce.

This concentration of land ownership, the lack of adequate and timely credit and technical assistance for small farmers, and a dependence on intermediaries, also known as "coyotes," at the markets have been some of the main causes of the injustices experienced in rural areas. These factors have engendered countless situations that have contributed to what the Latin American bishops have called the "structures of violence."

A ministry that does not, out of faith, confront these structures is out of step with history and becomes, as Marx said of religion, an "opiate" of the masses. The truth is that religion in and of itself cannot be an opiate. We are the ones who make it an opiate or not, depending on our "Christian" vision of the world and our commitment to our communities' existential reality.

# Land, Liberation, and Death Squads

Chencho Alas preaching in the Mirandilla community
Third man from right, Apolinario "Polín" Serrano, later martyred
Photo: Cornell Capa (1972)
International Center of Photography, NY City

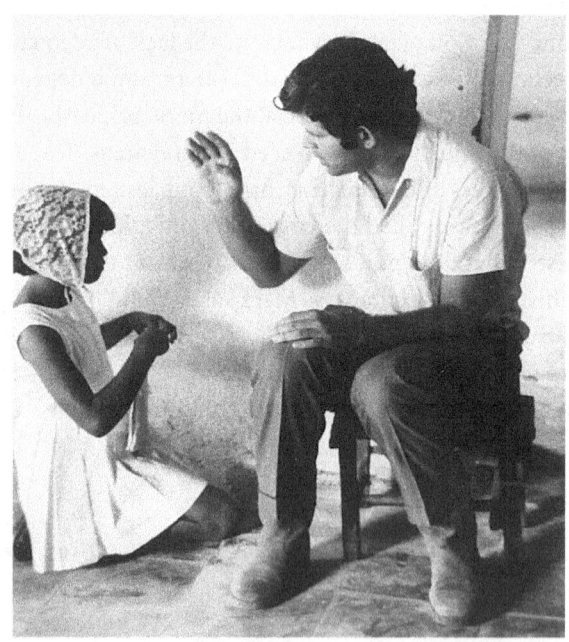

Chencho Alas celebrating the sacrament of reconciliation with a girl
Photo: Cornell Capa (1972)
International Center of Photography, NY City

## Leader Formation: Initiation to the Issue of Community

A month and half had passed since my temporary appointment to Santa Lucía parish in Suchitoto. The archbishop had told me the appointment was not final, so I had brought only the essentials: clothes, some books, and a hammock. I had no car, horse, bed, kitchen utensils, or other larger items. Neither did I have a plan of work for the parish. That was not a subject of study in the seminaries and universities. One assumes he is to give continuity to what already exists: liturgical celebrations; festivals; attention to the brotherhoods, to the young single women of the Association of the Daughters of Mary, to the married women of the Ladies of the Blessed Sacrament, and to the sick. I spent the end of 1968 peacefully; the only thing that worried me was the uncertainty of my future destiny.

It seemed my plan to work with Phillip Berryman and Manuel Cabrera, a Guatemalan, fellow students during my year at the Latin American Pastoral Institute (IPLA), was not going to come to pass. They immediately became established in assignments once they returned to their countries. Our plan was to put ourselves under the command of the archbishop of Panama, Monsignor Marcos McGrath, to provide pastoral workshops in the region. We had chosen McGrath because Phillip knew him and also due to his brilliant role in the Second Conference of the Latin American Bishops in Medellín, Colombia. McGrath was in charge of the opening speech introducing the subject of changes in the world and the church. Unfortunately, for various reasons, we could not carry out our plan to work together.

In January 1969, some kind of epidemic broke out in the parish, as well as in other places in the country. It was shigella, previously unknown in El Salvador. Children and adults were dying of incurable diarrhea, and I had to run from one end of the parish to the other to attend to the dying. January was an exhausting month for me and certainly featured nothing pleasant. It is not enjoyable to see people die without a doctor's attention, without medicines, with no place to go except to the cemetery. A few months later, I found out that shigella was a bacteria that had been strengthened in the laboratories of the Guatemalan military, with the assistance of the criminal and sinister US Central Intelligence Agency. It had been sprayed in the Petén to attack the pockets of guerrillas operating in that region. From there it had spread through the rest of Central America and southern Mexico. Once its origin was known, the appropriate doses were administered and the illness could be cured.

Towards the middle of January, I was asked to visit a sick man who was dying in Pepeistenango. By then I had my horse, a Thoroughbred-Morgan cross that Julio Rivera, who had been President of the republic from 1962 to 1967, had given me.[1] I mounted Piporro, the name I had given my horse at the suggestion of Julio's wife, Martita, and I left for Pepeistenango. It did not take me long to arrive at the sick man's small house. Piporro was robust, fast, and untiring with the youth of his five years.

The little house, like the majority of those in the area, was built of adobe, with a dirt floor and clay tile roof. One room, a corridor, and a kitchen; two chairs and a table as furniture—that was it. His wife greeted me, surrounded by their six children, who looked very sad. I greeted the neighbors who had gathered and entered the room to celebrate with the sick man the sacraments of Confession and Communion and to administer last rites. He was a man of forty, pale, reduced to bones by diarrhea and fever.

After completing ministrations to the sick man, I mounted my horse and started my return to Suchitoto. On the road I reflected upon those first weeks as parish priest. They were not at all encouraging. They did not inspire me; they seemed sad, monotonous, meaningless. I arrived at the Quezalapa River at dusk, and while the sun set, I was absorbed in thought, seated upon Piporro as he drank water. I asked myself what I should do. Suddenly I was hit with an inspiration, a revelation that changed the course of my life.

Clearly I could not do all the parish work on my own; it was impossible. Even if there were many fewer inhabitants, I would still not be able to do it. Instead, I needed to apply my theoretical knowledge learned at IPLA and other study centers. I must train people, leaders, who would then assume responsibility for many of the tasks for which I was non-essential. In truth, theologically speaking, a priest is indispensable for only a few but quite important tasks: to celebrate the sacraments of Eucharist and Confession. That is all.

---

1. The horse had been the army's flag bearer and came from the stables of the Guirolas, one of the Fourteen Families. Along with the horse, Rivera also gave me a hammock in which three people could comfortably sleep. It was beautiful, artistically decorated with the colors of the Salvadoran flag, and had been given to him by the hammock makers of Masaya, Nicaragua. My friendship with Julio Rivera had begun when he participated in cursillos de Cristiandad, no. 33 in Planes de Renderos in 1964. On the second day, around midnight, I met with Julio, and after talking about some personal things in his life, made him see that within his role as president was the need to improve people's lives, especially the campesinos' and workers', and to start an agrarian reform.

I wondered, as I admired the fan of colors of the setting sun unfolding before my eyes, why I might not invite campesinos from all the cantons to attend courses on the Bible, leadership, social issues, and other subjects of interest to their lives. I urged my horse onward, and with a whirlwind of ideas circling in my mind, I headed to my house, just four kilometers away. That night, I could not sleep; I was enthusiastic, happy. I thought that something good had to emerge from such an effort.

As I lay in bed, I thought about the subjects I would teach. I planned out visits to the cantons to select candidates for the first course. I determined dates, places, costs, and so forth. It could not be a short one-week course because I believed very little could be accomplished in such a brief time and I wanted results that would last. I thought if the campesinos had already harvested their crops, they would be fairly free, which meant they could take two months to study. Because they were so poor, I planned to feed them and give them six colones a week to buy beans, salt, and sugar to take to their homes on the weekend.

The next day, during the six o'clock morning mass, I spoke enthusiastically about my idea to the handful of parishioners who participated in the Eucharist. It seemed to me that their reaction was so positive—I could read it in their faces—that I dared to ask them for a substantial contribution to the costs I was going to incur. That very morning, before nine, I collected three hundred fifty colones: a lot of money! I decided to go right away to speak to the archbishop. I arrived at the archbishop's residence to be told that Monsignor Chávez had just left for the cathedral with Monsignor Rivera. I found them as they climbed the church steps. I begged Monsignor Chávez to give me a moment and right there I presented my idea in a nutshell. He became excited and, smiling, said, "I'll give you one thousand colones. Come to the archbishopric this afternoon to pick them up." Monsignor Chávez was a very approachable man; he was a true pastor. Now again I had something in my hands that excited me, allowing me to dream, to devote myself to it. People cannot live without visions that motivate them, without dreams that set achievable goals for them. I had found mine, and for that I felt happy.

I should note that when I arrived in Suchitoto, two parishes existed, Santa Lucía and El Calvario. But after speaking with Father Miranda, the pastor of the other parish, we agreed to form just one parish. In our division of labor, Miranda would work with youth, which pleased him.

That afternoon as I returned from San Salvador, I passed through the cantons of El Zapote, Haciendita, and Mirandilla, asking the leaders to convene their respective communities. I was going to visit them, one by one, that same week. I could not waste time if I wanted to give the first course that year. I knew it would take me at least twenty days to visit all the communities and select participants for my new pastoral adventure.

Suchitoto parish was ripe for the work I intended to carry out. Father Eduardo Alas, who later was named Bishop of Chalatenango, had worked intensely with the people on the subject of piety, based mainly in the Association of Adorers of the Holy Sacrament and other pious associations. It was an association of men thirsty for the Eucharist and for the word (lowercase "w") of the priest. The presentation they were given was pietistic, passive, underpinned by the concept of devotion of that time, which meant acceptance of the divine and the moral norms derived from that acceptance. It was an orientation based on the individual and God, God and the individual.

El Zapote was one of the cantons most often visited by Father Eduardo Alas. Because of this, I expected that it abounded in leaders. Located halfway up the Guazapa Hill, from its height there is a beautiful panoramic view of the Lempa River, of cultivated plains of sugarcane, the sugar mills, and beyond, to the north, the view of Chalatenango department and the first mountains of the neighboring country, Honduras. From the mountain's peak, San Salvador is visible to the south and beyond, the sea. The land of El Zapote has been excellent for growing beans. Today, Guazapa Hill has become a symbol of the Salvadoran people's struggle for having kept itself 90 percent free of all military oppression during the twelve years of war, despite all the efforts of the army and of its US military advisers to break its courage.

According to my schedule of visits to the cantons, about five o'clock in the afternoon I arrived at the El Zapote chapel, riding Piporro. Gradually people began to arrive. Some asked me to hear their confessions, and I went to sit in the confessional. My program for the night was the following: to talk about the changes in the world and the church; to meet in groups to discuss the issue and nominate candidates for the course; and to choose two leaders from among the nominees.

In a simple manner and with examples from their lives, I began to explain to them the subject of change. When I was a child, I told them, women wore ankle-length dresses that covered their bodies. That has changed; now women wear knee-length dresses, and young women even wear pants like us men. That is a change. Before, people got around on mules or horses, but now we use buses and cars. In the church, up until the Second Vatican Council, the sacraments were celebrated in Latin, but now we celebrate them in Spanish; when celebrating the Eucharist, the priest used to have his back to the people, now he faces them. Those are changes within the church.

Then I explained how lasting changes arise from within communities, not from outside. Hence, the importance of change agents, leaders. Human nature provides leaders in every community. For example, when a group of children plays, one of them immediately takes charge of the game, setting the rules, and the others follow him, unless there are more leaders in the group. Then I explained a leader's qualities or traits, the most important among them being service to the community, community acceptance, and serving as the head and not the tail within the community. A leader helps the community progress in ideas, values, and actions. Then I explained my interest in better preparing leaders about their faith. The community, better than anybody, knows its leaders; because of this, the community should elect leaders, through the presentation of candidates and a formal election.

At that time, the issue of women's liberation had not emerged among us. Religious leadership was a matter for men. Women were given a subordinate place in the church. This chauvinistic position has changed very little to date. In my short address that night I suggested that the men to be elected know how to read, because, among other things, they would proclaim the Word of God.

Once my presentation was over, the parishioners divided into groups of four to six persons. The children also formed their own groups. They discussed the issue of change and chose their candidates. Then there was an assembly to present the nominees' names, and finally, the election itself by vote.

There was much excitement on the assembly's part. My proposal had inspired them; they were enthusiastic. The idea of greater involvement in the church cheered them. They were especially surprised and interested in the idea that two of their community members would be able to distribute the Eucharist, to give Communion. That was certainly new for them. They would be the first laymen to give Communion in the country, and probably in all of Central America. This was, after all, only the beginning of 1969.

The next day I visited Mirandilla, and so on with the other communities. If I could meet with two communities in one day, I did so with pleasure. My enthusiasm was contagious. As time went on, I dreamed of the impact this group of laymen could have in the jurisdiction of Suchitoto and probably beyond its borders. Among other things, I thought about the formation of Christian Base Communities; these could give life to El Salvador. I had participated in one in Quito the year before as part of my pastoral practice required by IPLA.

Something beautiful happened during the presentation I made in Los Palitos, something which deserves to be remembered. The children participated enthusiastically, and when I approached one of their groups they told me they already had their candidate, and he was certainly going to win. They would not give me his name; it was their secret. When we began the assembly, they were the first to propose their candidate. It was Don Antonio Arteaga, a short, older man, very sociable and helpful. It seems the children adored him, because he paid them much attention. I asked him to come forward, and he excused himself; he could not read. Others were chosen instead.

In the end, I succeeded in finding nineteen people for the course. In some places, only one of the candidates accepted; in others, there were no adults who could read. Today, in retrospect, I think I did it wrong. A woman could have been the Celebrant of the Word. A child could have done the reading. However, practice is what allows us to start, correct, and move forward in many of our projects. Study centers give us only the ability to envision the idea we wish to carry out; practice is what leads us to achieve our goals. I have known students who have no head for practice; conversely, I have encountered men and women who shined in their practice although they did not excel in the classroom.

We began the course in the first days of February, as we had to finish no later than April 10. In April campesinos begin to prepare their fields. They know a campesino without a plot of corn and beans is a dead man for he will have no food for his family that year.

## The Community in the Dynamic of Revelation

The subject of the first course was the following: "The formation of the community in the dynamics of divine revelation." It dealt with achieving a clear idea of community, following step by step each book of Scripture, from Genesis to Revelation. I had researched this subject in depth during my year of study at the Lumen Vitae International Institute in Brussels. "Community" as a theme seemed very important to me for three reasons. First, the church is a community. Its founder, Jesus, conceived it this way, as a community of faith, hope, and love. Especially love, which is most needed. To believe is important, but we remember what the Apostle James says, "Do not forget that demons also believe, and tremble"[2]

A second reason is that the awareness that we are a community helps us understand that the country we belong to, in which we were born, is a community, or should be. That is to say, we speak of the political significance of community. This does not mean the negation of political parties. A set of principles and values having to do with the welfare of all, or what is called the common good, must exist. The concrete achievement of the common good is obtained through different strategies that are the product of ideologies. Political parties are the solidification of ideologies and their respective strategies. Political polarization into extremes is not beneficial to the majority. Political pluralism is necessary for democracy. Pluralism is not the same as political fragmentation.

This brings us to the logic of an economy in the service of all, because it desires the welfare of all, which is the third reason "community" is so central. There can be no hoarding of goods by a few if we believe that each community member is entitled to enjoy the assets of this planet, which has not been created by politicians, legislators, or by the most intelligent people, but rather by God. National assemblies should not pass laws about property, which God created for everyone, if those laws are detrimental to any of God's children. Private property is sacred insofar as it reflects God's holiness in creation, something diametrically opposed to selfishness, greed, oppression, and individualism. Private property is acceptable if it leads to greater dedication to the land so that it produces fruit of benefit to its owner and his or her community, whether local, national, or global. Abandoned private property is unacceptable; if the owner does not put it to work, others should.

With this in mind, I tried to present a theology of life, as opposed to a theology of books or knowledge. Theology must be rooted in history and revelation, so that it is a message and not a doctrine, since the Gospel is good news. This is the fundamental difference between theology and philosophy. Philosophy is doctrine, theology is message. Unfortunately, we

---

2. Jas 2:19.

easily stick with theology-doctrine, because it is colorless and odorless and thereby does not upset or disturb anyone.

The theological foundation I tried to present to the campesinos was inspired by the Second Vatican Council, my studies in the Institute of Brussels, my knowledge and practice of the liturgy, and, especially, by Medellín. The Second Conference of Latin American Bishops, celebrated in Medellín, Colombia, had particularly struck me. It must be remembered that Medellín's fundamental objective was to apply Vatican II's content to Latin America. I was mainly interested in the first two documents, titled "Justice and Peace." The message they offer is valuable, and the lines of action are important for pastoral activity that faces reality. Each of the sixteen documents from the conference is divided into three parts: facts of the Latin American situation, doctrinal foundation, and pastoral results. The connections between the Bible, Vatican II, and Medellín are tremendously powerful. In fact, in Latin America they gave rise to a new way of doing theology, the so-called liberation theology.

In the training we began to give in Suchitoto, we had courses in public speaking after dinner to end each day. This idea arose from a very interesting book written by Severo Martínez Peláez, a Guatemalan, titled *La patria del criollo*. In it, Martínez included an interpretative essay of Guatemalan reality, in which he provided an analytical commentary on the seventeenth-century chronicle *Recordación Florida* by the encomendero Don Antonio de Fuentes y Guzmán.[3] The part of that book that especially interested me was his reference to the pedagogy the conquistadores and their *criollo* descendants used with indigenous people to make them believe they could not think, and, therefore, could not speak, correctly. In my conversations with Salvadoran landowners and ranchers, I could see that they sustained the same assessment of campesinos, namely that they are lazy, immoral, and stupid, unable to express themselves; they are people without words. I therefore deemed it crucial to give them some public speaking techniques.

For these lessons, we chose one of the subjects studied that or previous days. We tried to brainstorm related ideas and facts. We organized the ideas and facts so they made an interesting explanation, then one or two of the campesinos gave a short speech. Finally, we critiqued the presentation. This

---

3. "*Encomenderos*" were individuals given grants from the Spanish crown to extract labor from indigenous people or peasants in return for participation in conquests or expeditions.

way, errors could be corrected and a mentality of questioning reality and fundamental doctrines was inspired.

In the beginning, it was a problem to get the parishioners to speak because of their lack of practice in doing so. They found it difficult to organize and present ideas. After two or three minutes they returned to their seats. At the end of the course, conversely, it was a problem to get them to stop speaking since they experienced much joy in presenting their thoughts to a small audience of their classmates. It was remarkable how they connected the Bible with reality, some with flowery language full of metaphors, and others in an unadorned, simple manner; in any case, they always linked their speeches with the facts of their own lives.

The campesino man's cultural universe is concrete, not abstract. From childhood he is used to working with materials, transforming them with his hands. His senses are highly developed. To understand the campesino's relationship with his environment, it is worth considering his relationship with corn. Before depositing the corn or bean seed in the furrow, he feels it in his hand, looks at it, admires it, and dreams of a lush corn and bean field in bloom. He uses his feet to cover the seeds. The plants have sprouted and are still very small when he clears them of weeds and fertilizes them. Once they have borne fruit, while the ear is tender, he makes atole from its grains, which is a family celebration, and later, once mature and the grains have dried, he transforms them into tortillas. The tortillas, patted out in the palms of the campesina woman, are produced in alchemy with her body, which works, sweats, tires, and gives life; they are the culmination of a whole process.[4] Therein lies corn's sacredness. It is work, food, life, the procreation of life, it is a gift from the gods or God. As a boy, I remember my mother forbidding me to cut a tortilla with a knife. I could not "injure" it, because it is a divine gift.

It is also nice to see campesino men in their games. In many cases they use their hands, their arms, to "fight" among themselves, as a way of having fun, without hitting or injuring one another. It is a way of communicating trust and joy. Their world is different from the world of the learned. It is a concrete world that at times becomes contemplative, as when Amadeo Acosta says to me on Guazapa Hill, "How divine is God who has given us daily bread!" as he admires his cornfield and the panorama before our eyes,

---

4. This is the reason handmade tortillas have much flavor and are so very different from machine-made tortillas.

a green carpet nurtured by the rain, sun, mother earth, and at night, nursed by the moon.

After two months of classes, of sleeping on the floor and eating beans and tortillas, we were wrapping up our first Celebrants of the Word course. Through their attendance, the nineteen campesino leaders had accepted the commitment of carrying out Celebrations of the Word every Sunday, giving Communion and working to organize their communities.

Before ending the course, we discussed the idea of having a celebration in one of the cantons. We planned to invite Monsignor Chávez and the parishioners. It had to be something big to mark the launch of a new kind of ministry. I went to invite Monsignor Chávez and he gladly accepted. We chose the chapel of Estanzuelas canton due to its easy access and location only four kilometers from Suchitoto. We selected two of the best speakers for the occasion.

It was an unforgettable day. The chapel was completely full, not a single person more could squeeze inside its four walls, and many had to participate from outside. Monsignor Chávez asked to attend without having an active role in the celebration, so I placed a chair close to the altar for him. It was the campesinos' turn to preside over the liturgy and Communion. The homily, eloquent and poetic, was given by Antonio Valte, who years later was massacred by the National Guard in the Suchitoto marketplace.

After the service, I asked Monsignor Chávez to offer some words to the congregation, to tell us what he thought of the observance and to bless our work's continuation. Monsignor was visibly moved, tears of happiness streaming from his eyes. For the first time in the history of the Catholic Church in El Salvador, campesinos with calloused hands and sun-beaten faces gave out the sacred bread; they gave Communion to other campesinos who with faith and love approached the table of unity and love.

From then on, we had masses in each of the cantons. The leaders participated in the celebration of the Eucharist on Sundays at five in the morning in Suchitoto; afterwards, they returned to their chapels, and in the afternoon or evening the community congregated. The leaders of Zapote, Haciendita, and Mirandilla, neighboring cantons, decided to take turns with the services, one Sunday in one canton, the next in another. Their form of celebrating the Word was certainly the best, as it became a fiesta. Three or four hundred campesinos would come down Guazapa Hill. They would assemble on the roadside at about two in the afternoon. When the leader who carried the hosts would arrive from Suchitoto, they would accompany him in a procession, singing psalms and songs of liberation. Songs with liberating lyrics have played an important role in the change processes in our countries; they have been an element that has gone hand in hand with our people's growing awareness.

## Origins of Christian Base Communities and Campesino Organization

As time passed, a new method of doing biblical readings in the services was introduced. Immediately after the readings, the congregation broke into groups of four or five persons and discussed the message among themselves. Then two or three small-group representatives were asked to present the opinions to the full group. Finally, the leader of the service summarized the exercise, motivating the participants to act. Sometimes the congregation decided upon a concrete action that the whole community would support. This way of discussing the biblical message gave rise to Christian Base Communities and their further development in Suchitoto. These were, to my knowledge, the first in the country.

With this method of work, new leaders emerged and the region's peasant organization developed rapidly, enabling further growth of existing organizations to address specific problems in the cantons, the districts, and the country. The obligation to work to organize their communities was intrinsic to the very concept of church we had studied, in accordance with Medellín's principles. The Latin American bishops had clearly proclaimed the need for intermediary organizations between the state and the individual in order to struggle for justice and peace—to use another word, for real democracy. In the bishops' justice document, the one that addresses the "organization of workers" and the "transformation of the countryside," the bishops affirmed that "intermediary associations are an indispensable vehicle to give the rural population access to society's assets, to culture, health, recreation, spiritual development, and participation in local decisions and those that affect the economy and national politics."[5]

By way of example, I will share an event that illustrates how Suchitoto's campesinos were in the process of developing new values in their lives related to the need to organize. They had entered into a new ethical vision of life, of their world of values. The inhabitants of Platanares invited

---

5. Latin American Episcopal Conference, "Medellín Documents: Justice," paragraph 14.

me to celebrate the Eucharist in one of their homes. Before beginning the service, several people approached me to confess, including a campesino about forty-five years old. As usual, he began in the traditional way, "Forgive me, Father, for I have sinned." I asked him what his sins were and he said, "I have sinned against love." To sin against love, in most cases, means the sexual abuse of a woman or a man, to be adulterous, and so on. I asked him to explain his sin and he said, "I have sinned against love, because I am not organized." His reply puzzled me. I did not expect it. I had not studied that kind of sin in morality coursework at the Gregorian Pontifical University of Rome, nor had I heard of it from the lips of the twentieth century's greatest professor of morality, Father Bernard Häring, at the Lumen Vitae Institute. My moral theology did not extend so far. I asked, "And why do you say you have sinned by not being organized?" His answer was swift and sure. "If I am not organized, it means I do not love my neighbor, that I do not care about my neighbor's life, that I am selfish." For that campesino and for many others, to organize is an obligation that has its roots in the commandment to love. It is an obligation that goes beyond political, economic, or social reasons.

That man's confession has remained engraved in my heart. God is the Community of three: the Father, the Son, and the Holy Spirit. They created man and woman to live in community, to be community. The selfish person's loneliness is not possible in God's heart. Those who do not believe in others, who are not in solidarity with others, are outside creation's plan. For that reason every form of individualism is sin, because it encloses a person in him- or herself, isolates him or her, and in most cases, makes him or her capable of oppressing others. That is the essence of capitalism.

It was, therefore, only natural that I soon began to hear rumors among Suchitoto's wealthy that I was indoctrinating campesinos in political matters. They claimed that a dangerous movement would arise if pastoral work fell into politicians' hands. In other words, something arose that I did not know about and did not expect: unknown eyes and ears carried out surveillance on our new ministry. This had not happened while I worked for El Salvador's wealthy, giving cursillos de Cristiandad.

Each month we held a leaders meeting in the rectory. The meetings began at seven in the evening and ended at four the next morning, in time for the early five o'clock mass. We tried to review the work done and the needs to be had. We also planned the services for the following three Sundays. It was these meetings that gave birth to most of the initiatives that turned

Suchitoto into an inspiration for other parishes and communities. In most meetings, it was a matter of clearly defining the problems, analyzing them from various angles, and then seeking and applying solutions. This method allowed for leaders' spiritual and intellectual growth, a deepening of their critical spirit, and very importantly, it moved discussion into practice so as to avoid theory for theory's sake.

At first we divided the parish into three diaconates or service areas, and we sometimes had special meetings with their leaders. The diaconate that functioned best was comprised of Mirandilla, El Zapote, and Haciendita. Their members were united and participated in their activities. I then believed that in the near future the church would allow the ordination of married men—in this case, campesinos—to be assisted and served by celibate priests. Pope Paul VI was a source of inspiration for many of us and we believed he was going to introduce major change in his church. That was not to be. With Paul VI's death, the inspiration behind Vatican II was lost, and we returned to Eurocentrism and Rome's hegemony.

## Chapter 5

# Land for the Campesinos and Genuine Christian Conversion

### Baptism, Sacrament of Christian Commitment

THE SUBJECT I HAD prepared to share with thirty-three new campesinos for 1970 was baptism. I could not begin this training, however, because on January 8 of that year I was kidnapped and had to leave the parish for several weeks.[1] By that time, a team of nuns of the Order of Discalced Carmelites had joined us, dedicated exclusively to our pastoral work. The Carmelites began the course on baptism, with Bernardo's and Tilo's support. As was the case with the first course, the communities chose the participants. After I returned to the parish, the first thing I did was to add my effort to that of the Carmelites.

It would seem that talking about baptism is simple. Not so. The doctrinal explanation can be given in a talk, especially if the reference is to the fact that through this sacrament we are converted into children of God and are "washed of our original sin," even if no one knows exactly what that sin is. But the subject matter changes once the concern shifts to the implications and commitments of being baptized. That was what we did, and that was why the course lasted two months.

Through the sacrament of baptism we join in participating in the church community, and we participate in Christ the priest, king, and prophet. That is, our new ecclesial nature requires us to exercise priestly, royal,

---

1. I will explain the kidnapping's details and aftermath in chapter 6.

and prophetic functions. I think these functions are generally unknown by Christians. That is because to exercise these duties is not easy; it can even be dangerous. We understand that these are actual roles, not symbolic or "spiritual," as is commonly maintained, to avoid onerous responsibilities.

The subject of baptism again takes up the issue of community, and does so in various ways, one of which is to make us a nation, a people. This message is crystal clear in its revelation. Saint Peter, in his first letter, tells us: "But you are not like that, for you are a chosen people. You are royal priests, a holy nation, God's very own possession. As a result, you can show others the goodness of God, for he called you out of the darkness into his wonderful light. 'Once you had no identity as a people; now you are God's people. Once you received no mercy; now you have received God's mercy.'"[2] Peter alludes to Exodus, one of the Old Testament's most important books, about preparing for the alliance between Yahweh and the Israelites. In Exodus 19:5, God says to Israel: "Now if you will obey me and keep my covenant, you will be my own special treasure from among all the peoples on earth."[3]

In the cultural anthropology courses I took in Quito, I learned we cannot separate the religious component from cultural institutions. The concept of a people appears in the Bible as a religious concept, but we cannot separate it out, rendering it distinct from the rest of an individual's or a community's life. What I mean by this is that the political, the economic, the religious, the family, the symbolic, entertainment and recreation, they all form a cultural whole of which the subject is the human being, man and woman. The concept of a people is found in the political sphere, which is also a fundamental part of religion. We need to understand these relationships, and even more importantly, understand their implications and consequences. To be church is to be a people of God while also belonging to a civil society, to which we bring human and faith-based values. In this way we understand that to be Christian is to be yeast in dough. The Salvadoran "dough" is oppressed, and, as Medellín says, must be liberated.

The full exercise of baptism, as priests, royals, and prophets, is our most perfect contribution to our own and others' liberation. Every minute, every hour, every day, a Christian should be a rebel, a nonconformist to the structures of sin, due to his or her baptism. But that is difficult! It is easier and seems more commendable to be a good Christian, a Christian of

---

2. 1 Pet 2:9–10 NLT.
3. Exod 19:5 NLT.

Christianity or, to use the language of the day, an "hallelujah charismatic" or member of Opus Dei.

With that group of campesinos in 1970 we first studied what it meant to be a priest. Naturally, there was no problem with this subject. The priest is consecrated to give thanks, for the *eu xaris* of Jesus's sacrifice and resurrection. Through baptism we participate in Jesus the priest; we do not need to be ordained. For this reason a couple celebrating their marriage celebrates it as a sacrament, because they are baptized. This is called the priesthood of the believers. Today no one opposes this priesthood.

Our second topic involved reflection on the meaning of being a prophet. This is complicated, perhaps the most difficult part of our baptism and the least practiced. It is complicated because the majority of prophets have had to suffer, to accept even martyrdom. Our country knows about this; it is soaked with our prophets' and martyrs' blood. That is why I have included in this book's pages a short chapter dedicated to Monsignor Óscar Romero, our prophet-bishop-martyr, the most illustrious of our thousands of martyrs, with whom I closely shared some crucial moments of his life and who gave me his generous friendship.

To be a prophet means to denounce the structures of sin and to announce the kingdom preached by Jesus. The problem lies in exposing sinful structures. Individual sin is not the same as social, collective, and structural sin, which have their roots in the political, economic, and social organization we have fashioned for ourselves, framed by a set of laws that do not always match the legality of the nation's structures and the common good. Our Legislative Assembly dictates the law, but behind the poor legislators with their patrician airs lie the country's masters, the oligarchs and the generals. The latter are masters because they wield the clubs and batons!

Legislation defines the political, economic, and social organization of the state and the people. One of the law's pivotal points concerns property. Ignacio Ellacuría writes, "People's destinies and characters as individuals and communities are at stake in property and its forms of ownership; it has been a key concern of great legislation."[4] The political, the economic, the social, even the religious, is organized around property and its ownership. By this, I do not mean that property is the end-all and be-all, but it has tremendous importance in life. Ellacuría tells us that "different forms of ownership have brought various benefits, but also great evils and injustices;

---

4. Ellacuria, "La historización del concepto de propiedad como principio de desideologización," 595.

something so essential to people's development and society's welfare cannot be left to the discretion of the most powerful individuals or groups. The issue of property has a fundamental ethical dimension; only by putting great effort into acquiring ethical theory and practice will we find an adequate solution."[5]

If the structure of ownership is unjust, if it is based upon the interests of a handful of individuals, everything else, like a river overflowing its banks, is bathed in the same type of injustice. This is what occurs in El Salvador. We need to prophetically condemn it, but to do so was, and is, extremely dangerous. I could speak to the campesinos from my own personal experience, having been kidnapped weeks earlier. I hope that one day our schools, when teaching local or global history, will teach the history of the prophets and not of the generals. There are battles that glorify the human spirit, which deeply touch people's longings for freedom, but these are not told; these are our prophets' battles, far better than those who plan death with killing machines, as do generals and the weapons they use.

The prophet is resurrected. Monsignor Romero said it well when he stated, "I have frequently been threatened with death. I should say that as a Christian I do not believe in death without resurrection; if they kill me, I will be reborn in the Salvadoran people."[6] Prophets believe in the resurrection; it is essential to their holy inspiration. How many of those baptized believe, feel, and live as prophets within our church? Few can answer in the affirmative.

Thirdly, we studied the meaning of being a monarch, which is also a difficult question. Sovereigns are free beings, and freedom is problematic. To be a royal means to be *dominus*, to be in charge, to have dominion. And how many have dominion today? Can we say that our country's campesinos are royals, in charge, free, if they do not possess one of the means to ensure their freedom, which is land? Can the person without work, without a fair salary, be in control? To which kingdom do our hungry children belong, those with extended bellies on whom we calmly sprinkle baptismal water, thinking that if they die the next day, we are sending them to heaven with little angel faces and wings?

---

5. Ibid, 595.

6. This is an extremely famous quotation that Romero gave to an editor of the Mexican periodical *Excelsior* just a few days prior to his assassination.

## Land, Liberation, and Death Squads

Right side, a campesino distributing the Holy Communion
Photo: Cornell Capa (1972)
International Center of Photography, NY City

Corn and beans, the main staple of our people
Photo: Rick Reinhard

## Baptism and Agrarian Reform

This subject—land—especially interested the thirty-three campesinos who participated in the course about baptism. Their pitched discussions contained the intensity of their lives. At the end of the course they asked that I add another week to study the subject of agrarian reform. Only through agrarian reform could they become landowners. Some of them were FECCAS members who liked to repeat that organization's slogan: "The land is for those who work it." I had studied this issue a little in Ecuador. That country's bishops were interested in carrying out agrarian reform on the land belonging to the Ecuadorian church, following in the footsteps of Chile's bishops, who had already done so. Monsignor Proaño, Bishop of Riobamba, Ecuador, one of Latin America's greatest bishops, was especially interested in this. For five days we studied the ten famous commandments for effective agrarian reform. We of course reviewed some statistics about land ownership in our country and in Suchitoto, naming by first and last names the area's principal landowners.

El Salvador is a country with enormous concentration of land in few hands. *Time* magazine introduced the legend of the Fourteen Families who own almost all of the country.[7] In reality, there are more than fourteen families, but that number, representing the country's fourteen political and geographical departments, gives a good idea of the accumulated wealth in the hands of merely a few people. The Fourteen Families are rich both inside and outside the country. A member of the Regalado Dueñas family told me she had greater wealth in the Antilles and New York than in El Salvador, and everyone in our tiny country knows how rich her family is. Most of the Fourteen Families, related to each other by blood or cronyism, such as being each other's godparents, are descendants of presidents. We mention only the Dueñas, the Regalados, the Quiñónezes as examples.

In El Salvador, 60 percent of the land belongs to 2 percent of the population. This land is dedicated to export products: coffee, sugar, cotton, and meat. Of the rural population, 96.3 percent own five or fewer hectares; in 1975, 58 percent of the population earned twenty-five colones or less per month. Thus it is easy to understand why 70 percent of children are malnourished and sixty of every one thousand children die before their first birthday. These figures, cold statistics, clearly tell us that ours is not a country of royalty, but rather of the "half-dead," as our poet Roque Dalton would say.

---

7. Hoeffel, "Eclipse of the Oligarchs."

Agrarian reform is primarily a political issue. The state's political will is first needed to carry it out in line with the people's will, after which there is the process of land redistribution. Without the active participation of the beneficiaries, agrarian reform will be like charity, which only increases poverty and dependence. In other words, to carry out agrarian reform, it is essential that the campesinos organize, defining why and for what they are organized. At its core, agrarian reform is not the result of a rightist or leftist party but of those who participate in it. To be kings, in control of the land, committed Christians must organize themselves. I believe this idea, which touches on the implications of baptism, became very clear to our campesinos leaders-elect and they made it their own; after that second course, campesino organization in Suchitoto grew more and more.

## The "Curulazo"

We got a tremendous surprise at the end of 1969. Dr. Juan Gregorio Guardado, president of the National Assembly, announced he would convene an agrarian reform congress, the first of its kind in the country's history. He invited the various associations of businesses, landowners, workers, and campesinos to participate with voice and vote in the congress. The Catholic Church was invited to participate, as were El Salvador's two universities, the National University and the José Simeón Cañas Central American University. The convening of this conference received the nickname the "*curulazo*." Within the National Conciliation Party (PCN), the party in power, there were tensions between those who favored reformist government policies and modernization of the economy and the conservatives, mostly agrarians, who defended the status quo to the hilt. These tensions existed even within families, between parents getting on in years and their children, who in large number had studied abroad. Dr. Guardado, supported by deputies of the opposition, took advantage of these tensions to convene the agrarian congress.

The curulazo had a political background. It was the result of the climate of dissatisfaction of that period, which had been slowly building, and weariness with the economic model of agro-exportation put in place in the late 1950s by the Economic Commission for Latin America and later supported by the Kennedy-sponsored Alliance for Progress. The model was supposed to generate self-sustaining growth in the Central American region. It was based primarily on the liberalization of markets and the coordination of plans among the region's agro-industrial, industrial, and commercial sectors. As always, workers and campesinos were most affected. These groups saw their incomes decrease year after year. In 1969, the rural per capita income was forty-five dollars per year. How can a person live on such meager earnings?

General Fidel Sánchez Hernández, elected president in 1967, had inherited from his predecessor, Colonel Julio Rivera, a series of strikes that indicated the economic and social uncertainty into which people had fallen. To some extent, during his last days in office Rivera wished to improve workers' circumstances, which led to an environment conducive to strikes. To this we must add the war between El Salvador and Honduras, from July 14 to 18, 1969, stupidly called by US journalists the "Soccer War" and by the Salvadoran military, the "Hundred Hours War," because it lasted no longer than that, given both countries' dearth of military equipment and munitions. It really was a market-control war between Hondurans and Salvadorans, the latter dubbed the "Phoenicians of Central America" because of their "greed." About three hundred thousand Salvadorans were living illegally in Honduras; they owned small grocery stores and other little merchant operations. Some had become owners of medium-size farms. Their exodus to Honduras had begun at the beginning of the century.

Honduras, meanwhile, the poorest member of the Central American Common Market, suffered all kinds of social pressures. Given its situation, it was looking for an outlet, and what could be better than to accuse the illegal Salvadoran of being an invader and try to have him thrown out of the country! The deportations happened propitiously, when the Canadian Paper Company was negotiating with the Honduran government for a thirty-year lease on pine forests in Olancho department, where many Salvadorans lived. The project came disguised as an agrarian reform program. The situation served to unleash virulent persecution of Salvadorans, who were forced to return to their country. The repression began at the time of a soccer game in Tegucigalpa between the Salvadoran and Honduran national teams during qualifying matches for the 1970 World Cup in Mexico. An estimated one hundred thousand Salvadorans were repatriated.

With the flood of returning migrants, the land pressure was felt immediately. General Fidel Sánchez, victorious in his war against Honduras, announced three reforms on September 15, Independence Day: agrarian, educational, and administrative. Nobody believed that the reforms were genuine. His announcement, however, created a favorable atmosphere in which campesino organizations could study agrarian reform and press for it. It was in this context that the curulazo, the call for an agrarian reform congress, was made.

## The First Agrarian Reform Congress

The opening session was vituperative. After Dr. Guardado's introduction, he gave the floor over to the participants, inviting a member of the National Association of Private Business (ANEP) to speak first. The member questioned the right of representation of some of those present, threatening that if everyone were entitled to vote to approve the conclusions and recommendations, ANEP would withdraw. After others spoke and with the majority of proposals contrary to ANEP, they decided to leave the Blue Room, the Assembly's session room.

Those of us who stayed more or less shared the same thinking, which caused the congress to lose political weight. After all, the time for agrarian reform had not arrived because the campesinos were not yet organized in large numbers. Agrarian reform had been one of the country's greatest needs in order to modernize its economy, begin a democratization process, and avoid an inevitable civil war of unpredictable consequences.

The first day's discussions clearly showed ANEP's main fear was a campesino insurrection. This was only natural, as peasants composed a large and inexpensive work force and, historically, all their rights had been trampled. When in one discussion I clearly mentioned the possibility of a popular uprising, ANEP member Antonio Rodríguez Porth immediately asked, "When do you think it will happen?" I replied, "Within two hundred years; that is, I do not know." To that the ANEP member commented, "If that is the case, we do not need to worry; by then we will all be dead." He did not understand my partly mocking response or, rather, he did not want to understand it. It was clear ANEP was afraid of this unanticipated congress, because we had a situation that could become explosive in the short- or medium-term.

## Agrarian Reform Beneficiaries

The congress's first day was dedicated to opening ceremonies and the organization of roundtables on various topics. I chose the discussion titled "Beneficiaries of Agrarian Reform." My interest in the topic was based on my mission, since in a rural parish it is not possible to envision a pastoral ministry that does not include as essential elements the land and those who work it, the campesinos, many of them members of various organizations.

The following day the discussions began. I was named secretary of the table. I recall that Dr. Fabio Castillo, rector of the National University, was at the table. There were also labor union representatives, among them one from the United Federation of Salvadoran Unions (FUSS). The talks went along in a normal way, without major disagreements. Nevertheless, when our work was at an advanced stage on Thursday, January 8, someone showed up with a tape recorder. We asked him why and he assured us that the order to record came from the Assembly president. This seemed suspicious to all of us and contrary to the freedom of expression that up until then we were supposedly enjoying. In a military regime, one gets used to suspecting everything, especially official recorders.

As is my wont, I voiced my opinion without weighing the consequences of what may ensue because of it. On that Thursday morning, I questioned the possibility of the government allowing those affected by agrarian reform to organize themselves, something fundamental to its success. We reminded ourselves that agrarian reform requires the political will of its beneficiaries. Reform is demanded; it is not given. To be successful, those who demand it should organize themselves in all matters relating to it.

My proposal at the table was that the campesinos form a political party with support from the middle class, especially from professionals interested in structural change. An alliance of campesinos, workers, intellectuals, and the middle class seemed to me appropriate, if not essential, as they would create a group whose main agenda would be the equitable redistribution of land. I did not suggest which ideology should guide such a party; in truth, I had no basis for giving my opinion on that.

The first negative reaction to my suggestion came from the FUSS members, who believed the communist party is called to such a task, and, of course, under the leadership of the proletariat. Still today I have yet to understand why in a country with an agricultural economy change should be made under workers' hegemony. To begin with, I still question the ability of the Salvadoran Communist Party, which remains in a rut when it comes to electoral and parliamentarian issues. The participant with the tape recorder smiled happily, as now he had probably gotten what he wanted. The sessions lasted all morning; in the afternoon we were free to work on our own tasks. As secretary of the table, I had been asked to return that afternoon to write up the conclusions which would then be presented the following day.

*Chapter 6*

# Kidnapped

### Fears and Capture

ON THE PIVOTAL DAY at the Agrarian Reform Congress, I had also made personal plans. At noon I had stayed to meet with Margarita Aguilar, a friend of mine ever since she was a child. We planned to lunch together and talk about her wedding engagement. Her friendship had always filled me with happiness. I saw her only rarely, because I was so busy in Suchitoto, and my interests were centered in the countryside, with the campesinos' fate. She picked me up in front of the cathedral under construction, located on the north side of Parque Barrios, next to the National Palace where the sessions were taking place. I noticed that Margarita seemed especially nervous and worried. I asked her if she was afraid to have lunch with me, and she said yes. Because of her distress, I requested that she take me to Colonia Scandia, located in the north of the city, where my mother lives. She agreed, mostly due to her friendship with me. She headed that way. Near Colonia Zacamil, noting her growing nervousness, which was spreading to me, I asked her to let me out in front of a bus station, which she did right away. I understood her while also feeling sorry for her. I did not know what a young lady of the Salvadoran high society could be afraid of.

    I got to the house and my mother, eternal slave to the kitchen, became alarmed upon seeing me. She asked me why I was returning now, and alone, if I had planned to have lunch with Margarita. I gave her some excuse that came to mind and I sat down to eat. She always had food for everybody. She is a tireless woman.

At two in the afternoon I again left the house, this time in my vehicle. At two-thirty, I needed to be at the National Palace to write up the conclusions with some of my colleagues. My mother asked me to be very careful. The comments she was hearing on the radio about agrarian reform did not please her. In fact they troubled her. The oligarchs were quite worried, and they did not mind forking over thousands and thousands of colones to the mass media to counteract the congress's purpose.

On the way, my mother's words kept ringing in my mind, as did the dream my friend Father Bernardo Boulang had told me about and Margarita's strange behavior. That very morning I had met with Bernardo at nine in front of the cathedral. He told me he had had a nightmare the night before. In his dream he had seen me attacked by a pair of National Guardsmen and he had had to defend me.

I arrived at the Parque Barrios parking lot, located in front of the National Palace and the cathedral. I was about to get out of the car when two individuals approached me, tape recorder and microphone in hand. They asked for an interview for one of the radio stations, though I do not remember which one. I did not suspect anything dangerous about the interviewers; I had already done some radio interviews during the congress, one of them that very morning. I asked that we do it right there, in the parking lot or in the palace. They told me they would prefer someplace else. I replied that it was not necessary.

In an instant, one of the two individuals on the steering-wheel side of my car moved the microphone close to me, as if to start the interview. In that split second, I knew I had to act. I do not know what happened, perhaps it was intuition, an apprehension, a sixth sense warning me of danger. What I do know is that I tried to grab the microphone from him, and I was left with only its silver cap. He pressed a button at the bottom of the microphone and it did not work. I understood, because his partner exclaimed, "Son of a bitch, now you have ruined our gas vaporizer!"

They tried to force me out of the vehicle. It was now not two but three individuals, one of them very tall and strong. Upon realizing they were attacking me from both sides of the car, I leaned back in the seat and with both legs repelled the one on the right while trying to defend myself from the two on the left. I lacked the strength and skill to defend myself, and they overpowered me. However, before letting them take me, I was able to bite the tallest one on his forearm. Part of his skin, full of hair, wound up stuck between my teeth, which gave me a very disagreeable sensation.

Distraught, helpless, I saw that the person responsible for selling parking lot tickets was running back and forth wanting to help me. It was Don Gonzalo Cáceres, an older man, a Suchitoto native, who had been given that job by the mayor's office. Don Gonzalo, a friend of mine, a recognized member of the opposition party, could do nothing. In front of me was a national policeman, who only smiled. I suppose he had been advised beforehand about what was going to happen. I lost a shoe and they forced me into a car, a North American model, after giving me a karate chop to the left temple. The blow debilitated me and almost made me pass out. It was two-thirty in the afternoon on Thursday, January 8, 1970. At that hour of the day, there were many witnesses in the park and people walking down the neighboring streets.

They whisked me away at high speed. I could not see the route they followed, because they had me face down on the car's floor with their boots on top of me. The position was physically and morally painful. I was wearing a Roman collar and it made me wonder what I meant to them, their knowing I was a Catholic priest. I felt one of them search my pockets for the wallet in which I carried only about ten dollars. As he pulled it out, I told him, "Look, I have only a little money. Do not keep it all; divide it among your friends." Right away they started demanding it from him. After all, they were rats of the same litter.

I supposed someone was following us on motorcycle, because one of them, probably the group leader, said, "It looks like that son of a bitch on the motorcycle is following us. If he stays behind us, take him out with a bullet. We cannot take risks." After a while, perhaps twenty minutes, I realized they were entering the premises of one of the security forces. I had my eyes half open. I saw a uniformed man, probably their boss. My captors asked him, "Is this who they want?" He said yes, with some distaste in his voice. Perhaps it did not feel very macho to have subdued a defenseless priest.

Immediately they moved me from the car to a jeep. I continued with my eyes closed. I felt that by doing so I avoided their hitting me unnecessarily. In the Jeep they put me face up, covered me with sacks, and then started the engine and sped away. Where were they taking me? I did not know. What were their intentions? I did not know that either.

## Acceptance of Death

The road was unending, or so it seemed. My body position in the Jeep was one of true torture; the floor was metal and I repeatedly banged my head against it on the bumpy dirt road they were taking. My head felt as if it were about to explode. I wondered if they were taking me to my death. I started to think about the values that motivated and inspired my faith, in the Way of the Cross I must accept.

During my student years, and afterward in my ministry as a priest, I had a great dedication to the liturgy. Its content and its symbols have always filled me with inspiration, happiness, and hope, and have constituted a beautiful instrument of liberation in my pastoral work. That day, I thought about Teilhard de Chardin, who asked God to let him die on Easter Sunday, a request he was granted. I thought about what the resurrection must be like, what was beyond death; about life, which by falling into the furrow becomes flower and fruit forever. I remembered the verse, "And where, O death, is thy victory . . ?"[1]

I thought of the campesinos, about those for whom I had struggled in these last months of my life. I was content to be able to suffer for them, to share their destiny; they are society's eternally oppressed and scorned. I thought about their land, which for them is life.

I did an inventory of my life, to those to whom I owed so much. I found I had failed in many things, but in others I had answered my vocational call. I felt happy, calm. I would not die in a bed, a victim of illness, but standing, in the struggle for a better world. To die like that seemed a dream, a gift I certainly did not deserve. To die for a just cause is not to die, it is to transform oneself into a symbol of that cause. That is why the blood of the martyrs flowers forever. To die like that is to succeed in having one's message escape one's body and run through the world sowing winds of hope, of liberty, of democracy, the purest and also the most utopian way to live out love in society. For that reason, all dictators commit a grave political error in creating martyrs, because in so doing they give more life to the ideals for which their victims died.

I thought about my mother. I felt her sadness and I also felt worthy of her. With my eyes closed I saw her walking through the house, always busy, tireless, small, fair-skinned, strong in spirit, a woman of prayer and faith. It

---

1. 1 Cor 15:55 KJV.

is a shame women are not accepted into the priesthood. They would do a better job of it than us men.

I accepted death. That made me happy. It gave me peace. I fell into a type of mystical sleep, which removed me from my current reality. Perhaps what was most difficult was the moment before accepting death. Once accepted, the nervousness, the anguish, the fear that invades body and soul dissolve. My tranquility was such that at one point my captors thought perhaps I really was dead. They talked about it and one of them put his hand to my chest to check if my heart was still beating. He realized I was alive. He even added a barracks-type comment: "The bastard's very quiet, but he's alive."

Photo of the kidnapping of Chencho Alas (January 8, 1970)
Photo: Diario CoLatino

**Harvesting Corn**

## You Do Not Have to Kill Him

We crept along a rough road. I realized we were passing the seashore, since I heard the sound of waves crashing against rocks on the coastline, and the heat inside the vehicle became asphyxiating. The proximity to the ocean worried me, because everyone in El Salvador knows that several of the neighboring cliffs have served on many occasions as places to dump dead or "disappeared" people.

The day advanced, and at nightfall they stopped in front of a *pupusería*.[2] One of them got out of the vehicle to order several *pupusas*, which they calmly ate along the way. For them all was normal; they were used to this type of work. They were professional assassins at the service of the security forces and of the government of the day. To clean their consciences, they only needed to get drunk, according to what a relative of one of my abductors later told me.

Every so often they communicated by radio with some center I was not familiar with, from which they received orders. The night was getting

---

2. A *pupusa* is a thick corn tortilla filled with meat, cheese, and/or beans, a very popular food in El Salvador. A *"pupusería"* is a small shop or stand at which pupusas are sold inexpensively, like a taco stand.

very cold. We had left the highway that snaked along the coast and we were probably climbing a mountain. I could not see, as they had their boots on my body and had blindfolded me. To mislead me, they made false comments about the places we were passing. They told me, "We are in Guatemala. We have known you have supported the Guatemalan guerrillas, Commander Turcios, and we are going to deliver you to the Guatemalan military. They will take charge of killing you; they know how to do it very well. They have no pity on people like you." The Guatemalan military was infamous as one of the most criminal forces on the continent. They had been trained by the CIA, by Israeli special forces, and by the militaries of the Southern Cone. It was well known that the Argentinian military had formed a school in Central America.

Suddenly, very late at night—I have no idea what time—my captors received the order to stop. A voice was heard over the radio, "We have reconsidered the situation; you do not have to execute him. Leave him where it is most convenient for you and give that son of a bitch a lesson." They went a little further, clearly up the mountain, because with each passing minute the cold became more intense. I certainly did not deserve the gift of martyrdom. That is a superior gift, reserved for very few people. I had to content myself with nothing more than a few hours of torture and blows to the head.

They stopped again and ordered me to sit, which I did. Now I knew they were not going to execute me. I was afraid of the lesson that awaited me at the hands of these torturers. I presumed it would not be a lecture or something similar. They were very short on words. They only told me, "This time we are going to forgive you, we are not going to kill you; next time you will not escape from our hands. Now drink this little bottle of alcohol. It will help you endure the cold, since it is freezing up here." I explained that I could not drink it because I have a duodenal ulcer and alcohol could kill me. "It is better that you drink it," one of them says. "Look, I am going to put this little pill in it; it is a drug, so that you get more benefit from it. In any case, if you do not drink it, then this will certainly put you to sleep." He held a pistol to my right temple and I felt its icy barrel. His tone was threatening and cold, like the weapon he was holding. I had no other choice. Right away I started to drink the alcohol. "That is how I like it," he added, "that you are obedient; with us nothing bad can happen to you." And he started to cut my hair with his knife.

Later I learned the change of order had come due to the pressure exerted on the government by Monsignors Chávez and Rivera, the auxiliary bishop. By Chávez's instruction, Rivera installed himself that night in the office of the defense minister, General Romero, later president of the republic, with the order to stay there until they had delivered me dead or alive. Later I had the opportunity to read Monsignor Rivera's statements about this to journalists. The bells of many churches in the country pealed all night, according to my friend and colleague Rutilio Sánchez. There had been an impromptu demonstration of campesinos, students, workers, professors, and some national assembly deputies and members of the Agrarian Reform Congress to protest my abduction. The people, with their civil and religious leaders at the head, had saved me.

Not twenty seconds had passed when I began to lose consciousness in a gentle manner, without pain or anguish. It was like entering into night without knowing the final outcome. It was probably midnight or later when I awoke from my sleep. Immediately I knew I was completely naked. I brought my hand to my face and realized I was vomiting. Waking up had been tranquil; it was like coming out of a deep sleep in a soft and peaceful way.

I tried to get up, but felt very weak. With tremendous effort I managed to get to my feet. When I tried to walk I realized I was on the edge of a cliff. They had left me in a drainage ditch at the side of the road. The sky was very starry, the night full of light, which allowed me to see the danger of my situation. A dry branch of a bush lay in front of me; I grabbed onto it and pushed myself backwards. This instinctive movement saved my life or at least prevented me from being disabled at the bottom of the precipice.

I lay down again and began to shiver. It was very cold, a cold that penetrated to the bone. It filled my body and soul, my entire being, a cold arising from my solitude and the night air at this time of year, in January. I realized there was "rabbit grass" around my body and I put some on top of me. To keep it from blowing away, I protected it with some branches that were at my side. And I fell asleep.

I do not know how much time passed; it could have been a lot or a little. I did not have a watch, as my captors had stolen it, and I did not know the paths of the stars. Very far in the distance I saw the gleam of a city. I wondered if it was San Salvador or Guatemala City. I must have been at a high altitude because the light appeared so visible and yet so distant.

I began to walk carefully, very slowly. I felt tired, weak, and the soles of my feet hurt with each step. One of my shoes had been left in the park in front of the cathedral, and they had probably thrown the other over the cliff. It is not easy for someone unused to it to walk barefoot. I advanced maybe a kilometer or more and realized I was in a dead end, or a "cul-de-sac," as the French would say. I had returned to the exact same spot. My initial idea had been to walk toward the light, toward the city lost in the distance, to walk until I arrived there or found someone who would have pity on me. I felt lost, defeated, disheartened, and especially without the strength to move forward.

I could not stay there, however. I decided to go the opposite way, toward the darkness. Little by little I began to go down, to descend from the summit. Now and then I saw campesino dwellings among the shadows, probably of tenant farmers on coffee plantations. Coffee, symbol of political, economic, and social power in El Salvador; coffee, symbol of land dispossession and the enslavement of our campesinos. Coffee was introduced in El Salvador in about 1865. Its origin is African. President Barrios believed it could be a potential source of wealth for the country. Laws were passed to favor its introduction and cultivation. Due to coffee, native Salvadorans lost their *ejidal* lands, and municipalities' communal lands were confiscated. Two decrees, one issued in 1880 and the other two years later, abolished ownership and use of cultivated land by Indians and the poor and gave it to the large farmers, who were sealed off in public administration or lived in the cities. This event constituted the first agrarian reform in my country, a liberal reform, which dispossessed of their land those who worked and lived on it. That began the immigration of many Salvadorans to Honduras and planted the roots of hunger and of future revolutions, among them that of 1932. All these ideas came into memory. Walking naked and barefoot, among coffee groves with their ripe red beans, I felt like a symbol of our people's nakedness, of their bare feet, with their sweat and blood spilled in the furrow of oppression.

I did not dare get close to the houses. I was afraid of the response I might receive from their occupants, who at that hour were sleeping, and from their dogs. In the countryside dogs abound, night watchmen, eternal guards, poorly paid and poorly fed. The campesinos' dogs, like the campesinos themselves, are skinny, their ribs sticking out. Campesinos eat tortillas and beans and their dogs eat only tortillas. At times it occurred to me that perhaps my captors might be in one of those houses. In such a situation, many things come to mind, some completely ludicrous and senseless.

Dawn awakened. I heard the song of roosters and early birds. I felt afraid of the day, safer in the darkness. One is alone at night and no one can see one's nakedness. When it seemed prudent to approach one of the houses, I decided to head to a small farmhouse. I had the impression it would be less dangerous, that its dwellers would have more compassion for me, more understanding.

I dragged myself along a narrow trail as best I could to one of them. I was exhausted and felt I might faint; I alternately walked and crawled. The door was still closed. With dread, I knocked softly and heard a little girl's voice saying, "Someone's knocking on the door." My heart was pounding. I wondered what they would think upon seeing the human wreck I had become. An elderly man opened the door. In the center of the room his wife was drinking coffee. In the countryside, the majority of campesinos, adult and children, do not drink milk. They have no cows, which cost a lot to buy, and they have no land to pasture them.

The woman fell motionless, her cup poised mid-air; she looked petrified. The man asked me to enter, and he signaled the girl to leave the room. Immediately I asked him where I was, whether in Guatemala or El Salvador. I asked if he had heard news on the radio of a priest who had been abducted yesterday. He said he had not. Campesino families have battery-powered transistor radios. The radio is their means of communication with the rest of the world, from hearing the news to listening to music, especially *ranchera*. After he replied, I told him I was Father José Chencho Alas, parish priest of Suchitoto, who had been abducted in San Salvador, in a crowded public plaza, the previous day. He just stared; he did not say anything. Then he offered me a cup of coffee. Their wood-burning stove was on the ground. The woman served me the coffee in a gourd. I happily took it and pressed it between my hands to feel its warmth, like someone does with a beloved.

It seemed the best coffee I had ever had in my life; each sip felt like fire penetrating my veins, like a caress to my gut. Then I asked him if he had anything I could put on to cover my nakedness. He said he had no clothes. I saw a henequen sack and begged him for it. Sacks are very useful to campesinos to store or transport grain. With a smile full of compassion he told me I could use it. In his face there was sadness. I asked him for a knife and cut the sack from one end to the other and across the bottom. I wrapped it around my waist. I also cut a piece to make myself some sandals, something to protect my feet, which were bleeding. Meanwhile the campesino had spoken with his son, a young man about eighteen, who had just entered the room. The young man then disappeared.

When I finished my gourd of coffee, I asked him the nearest town's name and distance. He said it was two kilometers away and called Jayaque. I started to say goodbye to him and his wife, but he suggested I wait a while and rest a bit more before I got on the road. He did not ask me to sit because there was no chair. I stammered a bit and stood like an idiot in the middle of the room. A few minutes later, he asked me to leave. In front of me stood two uniformed men, members of the local command. I felt the blood go to my head and I froze; boundless fear overwhelmed me. I felt betrayed by those who minutes before had offered me a gourd of coffee.

The two soldiers ordered me to come with them. They put me between them and began to walk rapidly. I found it hard to keep up with them. As we approached the town, groups of young men and women, machetes in hand, were going up the mountain. They were reapers of the gold grain, the coffee. In El Salvador the coffee harvest begins in October and ends in January. They saw me, looked at one another, crossed the street to get away from me, and commented, "He is crazy, maybe dangerous, because they are escorting him; and he has vomited on himself, maybe he is a drunk."

At the town entrance I saw the sign for the telephone exchange. Small towns have a phone center for public use. In some places it is the only telephone around. I ran toward it. My guards were surprised, but they did not prevent me. The center was run by a young man of medium height and light complexion. I told him I needed to communicate immediately with Monsignor Luis Chávez y González, Archbishop of San Salvador. In reply, he asked if I was Father Chencho. I said yes. He had heard that I had been kidnapped. Then, to my surprise, he added that he was from Las Vueltas, a little town in Chalatenango where my father had been born. His last name was Alvarenga, which meant we were probably relatives. He right away called Monsignor Chávez, who answered the phone himself.

The voice of the archbishop was friendly, affectionate. I could not hold back my tears and, sobbing, I told him where I was. Monsignor had not slept at all that night. He had done a vigil, awaiting my call in case I was alive. Monsignor was my pastor and friend. He asked me to go to the town's parish house and to wait for Monsignor Ricardo Urioste and Father Maeda, who were coming for me at once. Naturally the bishop's presence in a priest's work life is essential to his finding the necessary support, trust, and freedom to grow as a man and as a Christian in his ministry. Monsignor

Chávez was always a pastor to me, supporting me in all my pastoral initiatives, and he was a counselor in my difficult times.

The parish priest of Jayaque, who learned of my presence in town, awaited me. As soon as he saw how I looked, he hurried to help me. He gave me a pair of pants and a shirt that were both tight on me. He was a young, slender man, and I had put on some unnecessary pounds. After an hour Monsignor Urioste and Father Maeda arrived and asked me to accompany them to the archbishop's residence, where Monsignor Chávez was anxiously awaiting me.

Just as we were about to leave, a pair of National Guardsmen arrived at the priest's home. They told me that because I had been abducted, they had to question me, and that I should go with them to the Guard post to give a statement. I know the Guard. I know their roles as henchmen and torturers, and so I offered no resistance. I just went with them. After all, they were only asking for my statement about what had happened. At one point while they took notes, I asked if they had heard about my kidnapping. They said yes. I asked if they knew who my kidnappers were and they said they had no idea. Given their response, I let them know that I did know who the kidnappers were, that my abduction had been planned by their own boss, the infamous criminal and general Chele Medrano.

The drive to San Salvador became a long one for me. I felt deep anguish in my heart. I wondered about my mother, how she would be feeling, how she had spent the night. Finally I asked Urioste to take me first to her house; I wanted to see her, hug her, feel her arms around me. So he did. My mother's house was in the Colonia Scandia, almost to the outskirts of San Salvador, in front of the volcano of the same name. I rushed from the car and to the door. José, my stepfather, greeted me and told me my mother was at the archbishop's, that upon learning of my whereabouts, Monsignor Chávez had asked her to come to his residence.

A little disconcerted, I returned to the car and we headed to the Colonia Cinco de Noviembre. At that time, the archbishop's offices were located in that neighborhood, in an old house owned by the archdiocese that had been remodeled. As we arrived, several priests came out to greet us, which caused me deep emotion.

My mother was at Monsignor Chávez's side. When I was ordained a priest in Rome, in 1959, I did not get a hug from her. We were very far from one another, separated by an ocean. My mother did not have the means to be with me at that very important moment in my life. This time I had the whole of her in my arms. Her tears and my tears mingled in our love for one another, tears of happiness, of solace, of pain, and of hope. It hurt me to see her weary face, and I was filled with joy to see her mother's smile bursting with happiness. For her, my appearance was a rebirth, not of her uterus but of her prayers. She had been praying for me all night. The archbishop's face was full of happiness. His hug was the hug of a father, a brother, and a friend.

After these greetings, Monsignor Chávez asked me to go into the main room, because newspaper, radio, and television journalists were waiting for me. He warned me to be brief in my replies and not to accuse anybody. At that point there was no proof to accuse anyone in particular, although it was said aloud that elements of the government and oligarchy were behind my abduction. My involvement in the Congress of Agrarian Reform had worried them, as did my activities to help campesinos organize. They considered my work subversive to the existing order and therefore extremely dangerous to their stability and interests.

One of the journalists asked me what I was thinking while my captors had me kidnapped. My reply alluded to the reason for the kidnapping, although I presented it in the form of a parable. I felt, I told him, like I was in the basement of a luxurious home, a dark and foul-smelling basement. Above me in the living room, an assorted group of youth and adults were dancing to the sound of voluptuous music. While I suffered, they were enjoying themselves without caring about what was happening to me. Those who danced were the rich people whom I had served in past years in the cursillos de Cristianidad. A few days later, a woman friend of mine, a member of the Fourteen Families, phoned. Crying, she complained about my comment. She said, "We are not all like that. Some of us suffered with what happened, but we could not do anything about it." In other words, the existing oppressive structure is beyond the will of some individuals who would like to live in a just and peaceful world.

The press conference over, the archbishop invited me into the dining room. A big, bountiful table had been spread for some twenty guests, all of them fellow priests. They were my friends or those who in one way or another supported or appreciated my work. There I found my work partner Rutilio Sánchez, with whom I have maintained a long friendship, and who at that time had done both the possible and impossible to get me freed.

I had not finished lunch when I felt I might faint. My strength left my body, the same as it had the previous night, after having drunk the alcohol and awoken from my drugged sleep. I probably turned very pale, because after telling Monsignor Chávez how I was feeling, he asked me to go right then to see a doctor. During the cursillos period, I used to see Dr. Mejia Battle, who had his office at the emergency clinic. Father Nemesio Chinchilla, a priest from Chalatenango like me, took me there, and I was admitted on the spot.

My stay in the clinic was not pleasant. They kept me medicated almost all the time because I was having seizures that caused intense pain. My blood pressure lowered so much that by the third or fourth day a team of doctors thought I could die at any moment. Every day Father Chinchilla brought me Communion. Sometimes I took the host right away, but other times I felt so ill I asked him to leave it on the nightstand. Later the person who was taking care of me day and night served me Communion. My condition was so bad that some thought that if I did not die, at the minimum I would be mentally deranged, crazy. It took me about three months to partially recuperate.

On the eleventh day, the doctor discharged me. My friends thought it prudent that I not remain in San Salvador. It would be better to find some out-of-the-way place to recover. They offered me a house on the seashore, which I gratefully accepted. Staying with my mother and brothers and sisters on the beach, I received a visit from a priest with whom I did not have much of a relationship, due to our differing ideological viewpoints. I think it imprudent to give his name now. After asking me about my state of mind, he asked for my forgiveness. His request seemed strange and I asked him why he had made it. Then he told me something completely unknown to me and to many of us.

Chele Medrano, chief of the National Guard and official liaison with the CIA in El Salvador, met regularly with an informal group of priests—sometimes at the pool at National Guard headquarters, sometimes on farms—to discuss the archdiocese's ministry, which they maintained was infiltrated with communist ideas. This group comprised the religious front of the Nationalistic Democratic Organization (ORDEN). Several of the priests were military chaplains. The group's members were conservative priests, most of them little devoted to study. A priest who forgets his books is dangerous; his ignorance can cause a lot of damage due to his prestigious position in society. These conservative priests accused, by first and last names, the priests who followed Vatican II and Medellín. Later, in a clergy meeting presided over by the archbishop, attended by Bishop Aparicio of San Vicente, I denounced the group's existence and ORDEN's political crimes. Unfortunately, I was not listened to. A lot of blood could have been spared in the country if the bishops had denounced ORDEN in time.

## Nationalistic Democratic Organization (ORDEN)

ORDEN was founded in 1965, during Julio Rivera's presidency. One morning around five o'clock, still asleep in the Basilica of the Sacred Heart, of which I was parish priest, I received a call from Bertita, the president's wife. Weeping, she told me she had not slept all night. I asked her what had happened and she revealed to me the creation of ORDEN. Between sobs she said, "Our country, after last night's meeting, will be flooded with the blood of our people. Many will die; that is why I am crying. Last night was a curse for me."

That night a meeting had taken place in the house of Juan Wright, owner of the famous cotton plantation La Carrera. Participants included the president, various ministers, Chele Medrano, high-ranking officers, elements of the oligarchy, and civil servants of the US Embassy. The US Embassy has traditionally been the great midwife of criminals and terrorists in my country. The objective of those at the meeting was to create a paramilitary counterinsurgency organization, that is to say, ORDEN. They were there to discuss its structure, financing, and related matters.

The embassy's proposal was the creation of an organization similar to the Tagmata Ethnofylackha Amnyhs (TEA) of Greece, founded after World War II with US and British assistance. These were national defense forces organized for counterinsurgent purposes. Similar organizations were founded in Colombia with the assistance of General William Yarborough of the US Mobile Training Teams in 1960, and in 1962 in Guatemala. General Yarborough was the father of Latin America's "death squads." Our countries are rightly accused of backward politicians and dictators, but to find the fathers of these monsters we must not look within our borders but outside them, to Fort Bragg, North Carolina, or the Panama Canal Zone. The United States has too many Yarboroughs, paid criminal soldiers who cause too much damage to the world.

The training of these paramilitary organizations is done clandestinely by the army of the locale with US assistance. The objective is the identification of communists and their followers in each country, who must be denounced to the authorities, or, if there's not enough time, executed, as proclaimed by Major Roberto D'Aubuisson, Medrano's long-time lieutenant and certainly his best student. These paramilitary organizations were created as a covert armed wing of the counterinsurgency ideology of the CIA and the Pentagon. They formed part of a complete anticommunism strategy, which also included an economic arm, the Alliance for Progress.

In training courses in the barracks, ORDEN members were given a real brainwashing that instilled fear of communism as a threat to their lives, their possessions, and their religion. A priest knowledgeable about the Bible presented the part concerning religion. One of these priests later promised to get me the indoctrination manual. According to him, ORDEN's emblem had been drawn to represent symbols very familiar to Salvadorans: a shield with five volcanoes, a torch, and the colors of the flags of the country and the Vatican. He said the torch represented the lamp of the Holy Sacrament, which stays lit day and night.

During the first day of the religious arm of the training, Bible in hand, the priest explained to them the following: God has created all things; they are therefore sacred. Private property is part of God's creation and as such it is sacred, a necessary means to continue life on this planet. Whoever threatens private property threatens God, and it means he is an atheist. A good Christian, a believer in God, must be against atheists. Communists are atheists. They are our enemies. We must report them to the authorities. If the authority is not present, they must be executed. To kill a communist means to defend private property and constitutes an act of love to God. The leader of my kidnapping was an ORDEN liaison officer, under Medrano's direct orders.

When Julio Rivera ended his presidential term, he asked his successor, General Sánchez Hernández, to name him ambassador in Washington, DC. I visited Julio in the United States as I returned from a Laypersons Congress in Rome in 1967. He invited me for a stroll around the city. After walking for about an hour, he asked that we sit for a while in front of the Lincoln Memorial. Just the two of us, old friends, Julio began to look back on his years as president. He paused for several minutes before saying, "There is something I regret from my presidency, something I will regret for my entire life." He took a deep breath and added, "To have allowed the founding of ORDEN has been my worst error, my greatest sin. Much damage will come to the country on account of ORDEN." He knew its commanders and funders. He knew that with ORDEN's formation, death squads had officially been created.

When my spirit was sufficiently regained from my rest at the seashore, I returned to Suchitoto. I did it in the simplest way, as if nothing had happened. For my parishioners, however, I had become a hero. Some came to visit me to see if I was really alive. Some wept upon seeing me again, especially campesinos, whose simplicity is admirable, and their love infinite.

## Flying Again

One of the painful consequences for anyone who has endured abduction is fear—blind, unconscious, uncontrollable fear. A police officer, a soldier, a guard, the sound of wind blowing against a windowpane, even shrubs on a dark night may evoke thoughts of an abductor. Controlling these fears is not easy. It takes time and the return to work; in other words, it means facing reality, the reality of before and the current one.

A few days after my return to Suchitoto, Mario López and Mélida Anaya Montes visited and asked if I would give some talks on agrarian reform to the National Association of Salvadoran Educators (ANDES). Mario was secretary-general of ANDES. We had not known one another long but had formed a budding friendship. With time we would become close friends, companions in our ideals and struggles for the same cause, our people's liberation. I accepted the challenge they threw my way; it would be a springboard for my return to mental and physical normality and a way to deepen and expand my service to the people.

During my work with cursillos, from 1960 to 1967, I occasionally received pilot lessons to learn to fly small planes. José Noltenius, with whom I flew in his small plane, used to tell me, "If you have an accident and come out of it alive, get right back into flying. If not, insurmountable fear will overpower you." He made this comment after we endured a hailstorm while returning from Honduras, a storm so violent we almost lost our lives. I thought about José's lesson and told myself it was time to start flying again. Those who planned my kidnapping intended to cut off my wings. The effect on me was the opposite: with the abduction I achieved publicity that let me broaden and extend my wings in a nationwide flight.

Mario and Ana María were offering me that valuable opportunity, the "right time" Saint Paul speaks of, which if one values can serve as an opportunity to change the course of one's life or to drastically modify it. We promptly planned three conferences, the first in San Salvador, in the Teatro de Cámara. I would participate with Lito Menjivar, then rector of the National University.

I very nervously awaited the date of my national debut. I was nervous because I was not used to doing such things and nervous also about any consequences my participation might bring. My lecture's subject would be agrarian reform in El Salvador. When the day arrived, I asked my brother Sabino, a lawyer, to accompany me. The packed hall was standing-room only. As I made my way to the podium, the audience gave me a standing ovation. I felt small, very small, and at the same time it seemed my blood coursed through my veins like water gushing from a riverbed. It was a strange sensation.

When the lecture was over, my friends offered me a five-car escort back to Suchitoto, with the idea that along the way I should change vehicles. At home, Sabino told me that while I was giving my speech, two individuals in front of him commented, "We just beat up that son of a bitch and he is already talking again. Next time we will not leave him alive." It was clear that government agents were tailing me. Danger was ever present.

We had the second conference in the city of Santa Ana, in one of its theaters. This time I was escorted by a flotilla of sixty vehicles and policemen from city hall, then in the hands of the Christian Democratic Party. Someone had the necessary contacts to procure them. The policemen knew the government's secret agents or at least could easily identify them.

The third conference was supposed to take place in the city of San Miguel. The teachers were enthusiastic over the success of the two previous conferences, and they saw a growing movement of national attention to the public's most distressing problems. They were obviously interested in capitalizing upon this attention. I was serving this purpose, fully aware of what I was doing. The leaders knew that although change may be directed by specific individuals, in the end it is the organized masses who bring it about. Without the people, all change is precarious and short-lived. ANDES was seeking the organization of a mass movement.

This time, Monsignor Arturo Rivera Damas called me to his office. He was a calm man, an intellectual by nature. He was molded on a principle of Horace, the famous Roman poet who in a letter to the Pison brothers, says: "*In medio stat virtus* (Virtue lies in the middle)." Monsignor always looked for the middle ground. He said, "Look, Chencho, we have received a letter from Monsignor Álvarez, who tells us you are going to give a lecture in his diocese. He is worried about the consequences. We know what you are doing is right, but think about it, maybe it would be better if you did not go. You decide." Monsignor Álvarez was chaplain-general of the army. Some said that as chaplain he had converted himself to a colonel, instead of converting the colonels. He took part in political campaigns dressed in military uniform, and he had for a time a soldier as an office boy who answered the phone and attended to persons needing to visit the episcopal offices.

Monsignor Rivera Damas let me decide whether I would participate in the San Miguel lecture or not. His words left my head in a whirlwind. Pros and cons abounded. I knew what he was thinking, but Rivera was prudent and astute in not making the decision for me. He wanted me to decide on my own, which was fair. I ended up telling Mario I would not participate. I remember Mario's sad face. He did not pressure me, but neither was he pleased with my decision. He had offered me a three-hundred-car escort. In retrospect, I think I was wrong in not participating, that in so doing I sacrificed an opportunity to contribute positively in the push for agrarian reform. By not taking part, what I did was to ensure the interests of a bishop-servant to the army and oligarchy. They say opportunity only knocks once, and I lost out that time. The conference took place with a full theater. As a last resort, what they did was to present a recording of my speech in Santa Ana.

As a consequence of the kidnapping and to take precautionary measures, it occurred to Father Tilo that we should devise a way to rapidly alert the population if another grave incident happened in the parish. He got the Celebrants of the Word together and told them that if a similar situation were to occur, someone in each community should feverishly ring the church bells so that people could right away be on the scene in Suchitoto. Later, on the occasion of ANDES' second strike, we will see how very useful this arrangement was.

*Chapter 7*

# The Monsignor Luis Chávez y González School of Agriculture

### Origins of the School

THE MERE POSSESSION OF land is not enough. It is necessary to work it so it bears fruit, and tend it so as not to destroy the life it produces. In Genesis 2:15 we find that God, in giving the Garden of Eden to Adam, gives him a dual mandate: "to cultivate and care for it." Of course, the harvest will be greater if those who work the land know not only how to take advantage of the soil's resources, but also techniques guided by principles and values of respect for it. For this purpose, it occurred to me to found an agricultural school.

In the mid-1970s, Monsignor Colonese, who worked with Catholic Relief Services in the United States, visited me. He had heard about my abduction, of the pastoral work we were doing in Suchitoto, and he wanted to talk with me. At the end of the conversation, he asked if he could contribute money and, as to be expected, I answered, "Of course!" He handed me a check for ten thousand US dollars, which I did not expect.

For several weeks before this in our meetings with campesinos, we had been discussing how the majority of them lack knowledge of agricultural techniques. We said that if we had a school, we could train many young people, women and men, in agricultural knowledge. With money in hand, I thought such a school was indeed possible. We have only to buy land and build the school.

Someone mentioned that Víctor Escobar, my neighbor, had a piece of land on the banks of the Lempa River that he was selling. I did not waste time. I went to visit Victor and asked him to show me the plot he had for sale; naturally, beforehand I asked him how much he wanted for it. The check was burning a hole in my pocket; I believed very good use could be made of it. Victor quoted me a price of thirty thousand colones, or twelve thousand US dollars. I asked him to take me to see it, and that was what we did.

The parcel consisted of twenty-seven manzanas, eighteen of which were arable, including some six with good soil. A small ravine lay along the eastern boundary and there was a skimpy spring to the south. I asked Don Toribio Flamenco, an agricultural extension agent, to accompany me to see it and to tell me what he thought of it. Beforehand, of course, I told him I hoped to build a small school there.

Don Toribio Flamenco was a campesino from Caulote. He had a small fertilizer store and worked as an employee of the Ministry of Agriculture. He had no academic degree, but that did not matter; he was the area's best extension agent. He was friendly, a dreamer, a man of hard work and patience, and beloved by the campesinos. I was thinking that if he told me to buy it, I would. We went to see the land; Don Toribio not only advised me to make the purchase, but, like me, also began to dream of the rewards of such a school. I returned to Victor's house and offered him twenty-two thousand colones (eight thousand eight hundred US dollars). After some dickering, we settled on twenty-five thousand colones, which I paid him. That is to say, I spent all of the money Monsignor Colonese had given me.

Afterwards, I met with Eduardo Gavidia, an architect and old friend from the days of the cursillos de Cristiandad. I begged him to design a small agricultural school for me. I confessed right off that I had no money. After some hesitation, El Chele—that is what his friends called him—asked me how many students I would like to have. He picked up a pencil and a piece of paper and made me an acceptable design consisting of a large room for forty students, bathrooms, a dormitory for the teachers, and a wide hallway. I did not need to build a new kitchen because there was already an adobe house there, very old and spacious enough.

The following months were full of feverish activity. The only thing on my mind was the school's construction. I still do not know where I got the money, but the fact is I finished it in less than six months. Instead of buying cement blocks, we made them on site. Since I did not have a truck or pickup, I used my Jeep without a top to cart sand from the Quezalapa River a kilometer away. I scooped the sand from the river banks myself. I figured out where to acquire inexpensive lumber and went for it. I knew the Salesian fathers of Santa Tecla were dismantling some dorms and I bought windows and beds from them for a few *colones*.

At one point, someone told me that on Miramundo mountain, in the north of Chalatenango department, a landowner was selling cypress wood at a very low price. Without a second thought, I headed over there. Driving up the mountain was difficult; the road was unpaved and in very poor condition, but it did not frighten me. I finally arrived at the place, after having asked many people where the hacienda was. I was met by an armed guard at the entrance; since I was alone I was a little afraid. I asked if they sold lumber and who owned the hacienda. He replied that General Medrano was the owner. I asked if he was alone and he told me some two hundred young men and women also lived there, the majority of them "*cheles*" (North Americans).

He had not finished answering when I thrust my vehicle in reverse and full-throttled it out of there. General Medrano, that innocent angel of the National Guard! It turns out Medrano was sentenced to prison for a crime he had committed, and they had given him his own hacienda in Miramundo as his place of confinement. At his hacienda, Medrano had a marijuana crop that he consumed with his many guests. He had been the leader of ORDEN, the very organization responsible for my kidnapping at the beginning of the previous year. I had arrived at none other than the wolf's den, at the cave of the most cold-blooded assassin living in El Salvador, the great mentor of Major Roberto D'Aubuisson, founder and idol of ARENA.

Every school anywhere in the world has a name. I wondered what name could be given to ours. I spoke with friends and ended up naming it after our archbishop: the Monsignor Luis Chávez y González School of Agriculture. Why? For the simple reason that Monsignor Chávez always showed a great interest in El Salvador's campesinos, especially after a trip he took to Israel where he visited kibbutzim, which inspired him to found cooperatives in the archdiocese. Another reason was that many of us admired him and because I believed it was better to honor people while they were alive. Once they are dead, it does not give them joy.

# Land, Liberation, and Death Squads

**School of Agriculture Mons. Chávez and González**
**Founded by Chencho Alas**
**Photo: Chencho Alas**

After the school was built, my job was to recruit teachers. I did so with much anxiety, because I had no funds available. I spoke with Don Toribio Flamenco and he agreed to work for the school for a monthly salary of two hundred colones. Then I learned about two young men who had just finished their studies at the National School of Agriculture. They were Roberto Romero and Berty Orantes. I asked Don Toribio to accept the position of director, which he did without hesitation.

I went to San Salvador to visit some old friends, or so I believed them to be, owners of fortunes, who closed their doors when they heard my request for money. Among them, I spoke with Boris Ezerski, the husband of an Álvarez, owner of television's channel 2, whose only son I had baptized. He said with a scowl that he could not afford to care for his own employees, to whom he feels an obligation, much less for courses for campesinos. Fito Guirola gave me a *quintal*[1] of corn that he had in his garage and that was all. Tired and anxious, I went to the archbishopric, where I spoke with Monsignor Chávez. He asked, "And how much do you need?" He offered me a thousand colones, which I accepted. I returned to Suchitoto happy; with what the archbishop had given me I could begin classes.

---

1. A *quintal* is a quantity of dry measure; one quintal weighs one hundred pounds.

With Don Toribio we planned the first year-long course. I visited the cantons, and approximately thirty young men between the ages of eighteen and twenty-five were willing to study in the new agriculture school. We began classes in 1971. All was going well, but after three months, once the rains came, the young men started to complain. They had no shoes and their clothes were all rotten and could not take any more patches. Their families could not help them. Although the schooling was free, I was unable to cover all their needs. The communities contributed corn and beans, but they could not provide everything either. Under these circumstances we decided they could work in the morning with a salary allocated by the school and have their classes in the afternoon. That way they would be able to buy new clothing and shoes.

After the first six months, we faced another problem. To continue the program, the young men needed to know a little more math. Their knowledge was rather rudimentary; they barely knew the four operations. To learn how to mix feed, they needed the rule of three by four. Their academic preparation was too limited for them to deal with such matters. Berty and Roberto tried to help them, but the results fell short of our expectations. In the end we realized that a nine-month course was too long, and that it would be better to substantially shorten the next one.

The subjects we developed were divided into two main categories: agricultural issues and social issues. In regards to the first, we touched upon those topics a campesino needs, taking into account the diversity of crops and animals raised in our country. Our school's graduates should have been able to manage a farm of ten to fifteen manzanas and have the methodology needed to transmit agricultural knowledge to other campesinos. Our interest was to turn out of our school a campesino who would serve as a bridge between the agronomist and traditional farm worker.

Regarding social issues, we needed a young campesino with the knowledge required to develop his leadership and the ability to analyze his milieu. He needed to analyze our national reality and our country's dependency on international powers. We did not want a campesino who was at the tail, one of the masses, but someone who was a guide, a leader, who knew how to organize his *compañeros*. As this matter was of special interest to Father Bernardo Boulang, he teamed up with us for some months.

As to be expected, criticisms and accusations soon began from National Conciliation Party members, led by Pepe Rivera, employee of the Presidential House, and by the city's mayor and his whole choir of incompetent brown-nosers. One day two military men appeared at the school. I was teaching a class, which I interrupted to attend to them. They told me they had come in the name of President Molina, who was elected president, through fraud, in 1972. I still remember one of their names: Captain Mauricio Vides Casanova. Molina was inviting me to a very private meeting on a farm in Apopa. He wanted no witnesses. He had already met with some priests, among them Father Roberto Trejos, and he wanted to talk with me about social issues. Molina knew his support base was minimal, that he had been elected fraudulently, and he wanted to improve his own and the army's political standing with the people. As to be expected, I refused to participate because I thought the meeting's objective was outside the purview of my role.

Captain Vides Casanova was annoyed by my reply. It seemed strange and rude to him. I simply invited him to look around and get to know the small school. There were two huge cement slabs near the building; he stopped at them and said, "We know small planes fly by here and drop packages. We know they are weapons. Are the weapons stored beneath these enormous slabs?" I replied, "Yes, they are there. To be sure of it, I invite you, with the students' help, to remove the slabs and to go down there to verify the weapons' existence. After you go down, you are going to come out with your clothes the color of cappuccino." Baffled, he asked, "Why that color?" I answered bluntly, "Because they will be the color of shit. Those are two septic tanks." The captain's face turned blood red he was so angry. But I was even angrier that they accused us of storing weapons there. That would be endangering innocent young people for no purpose.

To end our first course we decided to have a nice closing ceremony with speeches, music, and food. As imagined, those who should have had front-row seats were the area's campesinos. So we issued a come-all invitation to the communities. We prepared as well as possible, even killing a young bull that Don Ramón Arteaga had given me. He gave it to me because it was covered with sores and condemned to die. What the little animal needed was food and good treatment. After several months of grazing on the school's fields, he had grown nice and fat.

The Celebrants of the Word wanted to participate in the ceremony with their own one-act play, a comedy. I was aware that they were practicing, but I did not know what they were going to present. The day arrived, and we saw some of them dressed as military men, others as priests, and one as a bishop. The subject was not the church-military alliance, but rather certain church members' submission to the military. It was a comedy of censure. As might be expected, the audience roundly applauded them.

## THE MONSIGNOR CHÁVEZ Y GONZÁLEZ SCHOOL OF AGRICULTURE

Hunger has a child's face in El Salvador
Photo: Cornell Capa (1972)
International Center of Photography, NY City

## New Courses

After the first experience, we discussed the content and methodology to implement during the second year. We decided the courses should last only three months and must be oriented to agricultural practices. In addition, we considered courses for young women, to be focused on their interest in raising small animals and kitchen crops. Women often put a lot of care in raising small animals, and they are interested in growing crops that require intensive care such as vegetables.

These courses also turned out to be too long, and we decided to reduce them to two weeks, one week at the school and the other in the communities. By then we were raising hay, rice, sugarcane, vegetables, and other crops at the school. We were equipped with a truck, a tractor, and a small irrigation system; additionally, we had introduced several kinds of animals. We had cattle, horses, pigs, chickens, rabbits, and even a male and female goat given to me by Father Stanley Rother, a North American who worked in Santiago Atitlán, Guatemala. The male goat came from Boston and the female had been born in Switzerland and was very good for milk. Years later while visiting Oklahoma, I learned that Father Stanley was assassinated by the Guatemalan army. He had to have been a very good priest.

Agriculture courses were certainly necessary for campesinos, but they left a still up-in-the-air question we had to answer: by any chance do the campesinos have land? How many would be able to apply their new knowledge on a little plot of their own? The answer was very few. So then who were we working for? In other words, our thinking led us to the need to study and organize to demand land reform from the government.

## Other Activities

We used the school for many other activities as well. Every two weeks we met in it with the Celebrants of the Word to prepare them for their preaching and the work of organizing their communities. It served me personally as a place of rest. With its views of the Lempa River and the Chalatenango mountains, it was a nice place to get away and rest or to spend time caring for the animals.

The animals were a constant source of joy and relaxation. We knew in advance the animals were not able to criticize us or their fellow animal companions. I will always remember Yanko, an enormous seven-hundred-pound hog who won me two national prizes. He would hardly hear my voice and he became restless; he wanted to see me and be petted. When I got to his pen, he stood on his hind legs, waiting for me to pet his head. The countryside teaches us much more than we think.

## The End of the School

They say good things end quickly. The school did not last long; it came to an end after five years. With the construction of the Cerrón Grande dam, the school was flooded at the end of 1976. I was able to get the Lempa Energy Company (CEL) to pay me one hundred five thousand colones. In a first appraisal, they had offered sixty-five thousand colones, which of course I did not accept. By then, a group of campesinos from Los Palitos wanted to relocate together, in a collectivized cooperative. Most were members of FECCAS with solid experience in organizing. I joined them and gave them seventy-five thousand colones of the funds I had received from the Lempa Energy Company. The remaining funds helped me pay my debts. Our school's most enduring benefit was being able to rely on a fairly large number of young people familiar with social analysis and willing to organize themselves for the work of the country's liberation.

*Chapter 8*

# The Capture of Thirty-Seven ANDES Teachers

THE POPULATION OF SUCHITOTO had learned to organize to such an extent that it had achieved a level of true sophistication. The following fact is the best proof of this assertion. In June 1971, ANDES had its second strike. Walter Beneke was the Minister of Education; prior to taking that post he had been ambassador to Japan. He was arrogant and stubborn, and refused to dialogue with the teachers. In response, they began a strike that lasted several months. ANDES received support from all the organized grassroots groups: workers, campesinos, market women, opposition party activists, and others. As to be expected, the government unleashed repression across the country; many were persecuted, imprisoned, and, in some cases, tortured.

In Suchitoto, we got ready to support the teachers and we organized various assistance activities. All the district's teachers were on strike and we decided to stand alongside them. In this context, it happened that thirty-three teachers from Cojutepeque decided to visit Suchitoto's teachers to encourage them. They hired a bus to travel together. Suchitoto's National Guard learned of the teachers' arrival, and went out to meet them near the entrance to Ichanqueso, some seven kilometers from Suchitoto. They ordered the driver to stop, and after having seized what they were carrying, they confiscated some newspapers published that morning, among them *Diario de Hoy* of the ultraconservative Viera Altamirano. They ordered the driver to follow them, and they took them all on board to the town jail, which is next to city hall.

I was in San Salvador, participating in a meeting chaired by Monsignor Arturo Rivera Damas, president of the Liturgy Commission of which

## THE CAPTURE OF THIRTY-SEVEN ANDES TEACHERS

I was a member. When I returned to town, I found a group of local teachers and friends, among them Omar Alas, in front of the jail chanting slogans and singing to encourage their friends. I stopped and asked them what was going on. Omar told me, "The Guard has arrested the teachers who were coming from Cojutepeque to support our teachers. But they are not the only prisoners; they have also locked up four of our teachers who, upon realizing what was happening to the visitors, went out to see how they could help them. Among our teachers are my wife and Chita Durán. There are thirty-seven in the slammer."

I asked him what they planned to do and he replied, "We are here to encourage them and to watch what happens. If they take them to San Salvador, we will follow; we cannot leave them alone." I asked, "Will that be enough? Can anything more be done?" Omar shook his head and had no answer. I asked that four of them come to my house, and while I lunched we could brainstorm what else could be done. We had to free those people before they were taken to San Salvador.

While I ate, we advanced the following dialogue, in which Omar especially participated. He asked, "Should we send a delegation to San Salvador to let the strike's Central Committee know what has happened? Should we call the radio to denounce what has happened?"

I proposed something wild, but possible. "How about we have a mass tonight?"

They laughed and said, "Why a mass? How can it help the imprisoned?"

"It can help if many people attend," I responded. "In the preaching I can mention every citizen's right to demonstrate and after the mass we can have a march."

"It is three in the afternoon, a mass at seven and then a demonstration . . . It cannot be done; it is very late."

"Yes, it's possible. You invite the townspeople and I will invite the campesinos."

They puzzled, "And how are you going to invite the campesinos now? It is late and there is no transportation, so they will not come."

"That is my problem. I will figure it out, but you invite the townspeople."

"Let's do it then," Omar said. "Come on. You go to the countryside and we'll go to the city."

I immediately climbed into my Jeep and went to the agricultural school. We were then giving a course to a group of forty young men. I went immediately to Don Toribio Flamenco, the director, and asked that he let me have some fifteen young men to go to the cantons.

He asked me, naturally, what was going on, and I told him of the teachers who had been imprisoned and that we must find a way to free them. At once we asked for fifteen volunteers, and as might be expected, all of them wanted to go. I asked six of them who knew how to ride a horse to go to an equal number of cantons; the rest came with me. I instructed them on their mission, which was very simply to ring the cantons' church bells like mad and to talk with the first people they saw in order to convey our sense of urgency. What was happening in Suchitoto was urgent and we needed immediate support.

At seven in the evening we had a huge crowd in Suchitoto. We rang the church bells and then began the celebration of the mystery of life, the sacred Eucharist. The preaching, as anticipated, was intended to give hope to the struggles we were undertaking in the name of justice. Before ending the mass I announced that there would be a march through the city and that it was very important that everyone participate. We must demand the freedom of our innocent teachers.

Once outside the church, the Celebrants of the Word and a good number of teachers quickly tried to organize the crowd to begin the march. According to our plan, we were to head to the El Calvario neighborhood at the city's main entrance, passing in front of the jail, and then on to the Concepción neighborhood in the north of Suchitoto. We wanted to cross the city from one end to the other. Finally, we planned to place ourselves in front of the jail, all night if necessary.

As the people formed into groups of ten, occupying the whole street, more people from both countryside and city joined. Those lines were endless. After passing in front of the jail, we made it to the National Guard headquarters. I stared at the entrance and noticed with surprise that it was closed. What was going on? Were they afraid? When we got to Gallardos, I asked Toño Valte and Amadeo Acosta to count the participants. The operation was simple: just count the number of lines and multiply by ten. After an hour or so they returned and said, "We have about ten thousand people marching here." Then I understood why the Guards had shut the door. They *were* simply afraid!

One of the first demonstrations of teachers
Photo: Free Images

The face of poverty
Photo: Rick Reinhard

The atmosphere was one of joy; it was triumphant. People sang, shouted slogans, encouraged one another. And, of course, we were all truly surprised to find so many in this march that was organized so quickly!

Having completed our planned route, we headed to the jail. There the people's enthusiasm heated up. Some belted out the names of the locked-up teachers, encouraging them, infusing them with joy and hope for freedom. Others danced. Since the jail door was shut, we could not see what was going on inside. Only later did we learn that the prisoners were also holding their own rally in the jail's courtyard.

We did not sleep that night. Some brought firewood from their own homes and soon we had a nice campfire going. Some women realized it was a good time to make a few cents, and three or four of them appeared with their little stoves, oil, plantains, and other things to sell food to those of us who had remained to do vigil, some four hundred persons. Our Salvadoran women never miss a chance to earn a little. The night air was cool and although we were tired, our joy was deep. We stood with an organized people. Tilo Sánchez was right to organize a system of rapid mobilization, to deploy it whenever needed.

At about five in the morning the judge arrived at the jail and ordered that the teachers come out in groups of five, accompanied by their guards, so as to give them a brief trial. As anticipated, there was no reason to keep them imprisoned. The Guards had simply exceeded their power. As they almost always did! At eleven in the morning all of the teachers had gone through a trial and were free. No one, however, had left. Everyone awaited the final result, to see that all were freed. At that point Omar arrived at my house and said, "Now we want a *Te Deum* (St. Augustine and St. Ambrosio's hymn of thanksgiving). We want it, but very solemn."

The day before, in the afternoon, we had gotten the prison guards to let us to pass woven-palm mats to the imprisoned. So as they left the jail, they carried their outspread mats. Although the crowd was no longer as large as the night before, many people came together for that *Te Deum* of freedom.

A few days later I met with René Glower Valdivieso, who used to be Chita Durán's boyfriend, and he told me he had managed to enter the Guard post, because he had been a cadet in the military school. He told me the Guards had trembled with fear. The commander of the Guard had since installed radio communication with headquarters and increased the number of the garrison's members. This was to be expected.

*Chapter 9*

# Presidential Elections
*The Nuncio and the Guards*

### Pre- and Post-Election Atmosphere

THE ELECTION OF ARTURO Armando Molina to the presidency in 1972 was plagued by events that affected the Church's already poor relations with the government. These surrounding events expressed the government's growing despair over a church increasingly less allied with the powerful. During election campaigns it was traditional for candidates, upon arrival in a town, to visit the parish church and deposit a floral bouquet at the patron saint's statue and a hundred or so colones in alms. Then they would give their speeches.

On Sunday, January 17, 1972, one of the main pillars of Suchitoto's small-town politics visited me to let me know Colonel Molina would hold his meeting that day. He asked that I at least leave the church doors open so that the military officer could visit Saint Lucía and present his offerings to her. Besides, he added with a sardonic smile, Molina had a nice personal check prepared for me for my personal expenses and he wanted me to receive it at the altar. I asked him if Molina was visiting Saint Lucía to fulfill a religious promise because of eye problems—Saint Lucía is the patron saint of vision—or if it was to carry out partisan politics under the protection of our bell tower. If it was the former, he had the right to enter the church and pray like any Christian. If it was the latter, I proposed two alternatives: first, that he not enter the church at all; or, second, if he did enter that he then visit all the city's churches, including the evangelical churches. At that time, the evangelical population was very small.

At two in the afternoon the presidential candidate arrived in the city. Knowing my way of thinking, he did not dare enter the church. However, my brother Higinio and Bernardo Boulang wanted to hear his political spiel and to even record it for later analysis with the campesinos. Prior to Molina's arrival, they had positioned themselves in the choir of the church, a strategic place from which they could hear the speeches and see the candidates. Mayorga Rivas, whom I led in cursillos de Cristiandad instruction, accompanied Molina as candidate for vice president.

As expected, at some point they directed their speeches against us for our work on behalf of the campesinos. As usual in these cases, they called us wolves dressed in sheepskin who shamelessly supported communists, acted contrary to democracy, and so forth. Someone in their entourage learned of Higinio and Bernardo's presence in the choir and they informed the heavily armed police accompanying the candidates. Immediately, the police busted the church door open, closed as usual at that hour, went to the choir, and, wielding bayonets with an excess of barbarity, removed the two priests from the church. The event took place at the very moment in which the candidate was proclaiming his respect, love, and support of the church, pope, bishops, priests, and the Catholic Salvadoran people. This abuse was not isolated; similar events had occurred in San Juan Opico in the department of La Libertad, and in Ojos de Agua in the department of Chalatenango.

A few days later a group of the most active priests met in San Salvador. We analyzed the acts of violence against civilian and religious figures and decided to denounce them publicly. To give greater import to our criticism, we wrote a proclamation and asked that it be signed by the largest possible number of priests in the country. Father Benito Tovar and I visited some twenty parishes and we asked their priests to sign our document. We arrived at a certain parish in Santa Ana at two in the morning. The priest was sound asleep, as expected. We woke him, explained our mission, and asked for his signature. He was a young priest, who made himself out to be very liberal. He did not sign; however, other priests we considered conservative did not hesitate to sign. We got a total of sixty-three signatures. In our proclamation, we condemned all abuses, those already committed as well as those to come, and we affirmed, according to canon law, that to strike a priest unjustly can cause excommunication. We made the proclamation public three days before Election Day. The impact, as anticipated, was tremendous.

Later I learned directly from attorney Vicente Vilanova, the election commission president, that Molina lost the elections, and by a very large margin. To prevent the departure of the military from power, Vilanova himself had to concoct electoral fraud. After phoning Molina, he stopped the vote count late in the night; the following day, Molina magically led the other candidates. Vilanova explained to me that Napoleón Duarte's arrival in power would have signified the entry of communists in to government. Duarte was the favorite candidate of the people, as well as of some military personnel.

Campesinos going to a demonstration
Photo: Cornell Capa (1972)
International Center of Photography, NY City

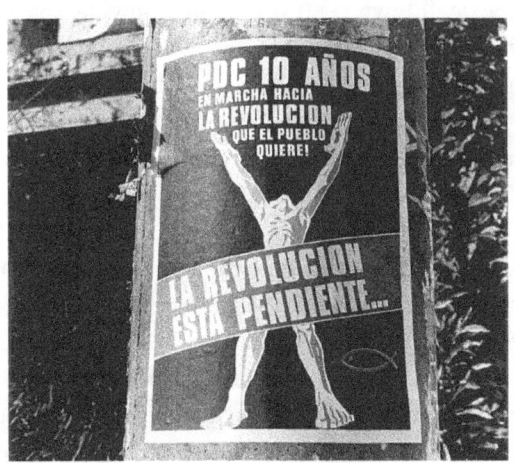

Electoral campaign
Photo: Cornell Capa (1972)
International Center of Photography, NY City

## The Nuncio Intervenes

Our activities worried the nuncio Emmanuelle Gerada, the Vatican's ambassador to the Salvadoran government. In 1972, he took advantage of a meeting of the priests of Quetzaltepeque and San Bartolomé Perulapía vicariates in Domus Mariae. Diplomatically and with Monsignor Chávez's permission, he spoke to us of his vision of the church. Naturally it was a diplomat's vision, rather than of a theologian or pastor, the vision of a man committed to alliances with established powers. We listened to him with respect, a score of parish priests. We asked some questions and made some comments, and at the end he expressed interest in visiting our towns. I spoke up and asked him to visit Suchitoto. Of course, I was not interested in his visiting the town but rather some campesino communities. He accepted, which I admired and with which I was pleased.

At that time, in 1972, those of us working in Suchitoto included Bernardo Boulang, Jesús Ángel Bengochea, a Jesuit, my brother and I. On the designated Sunday, the nuncio arrived in Suchitoto. Monsignor Gerada was a very formal, elegant man, who on that occasion wore a white cassock with its ornamentation like a bishop's vestments. His manner was easy, pleasant, and he seemed happy to be in the countryside, out of the city and of his palace built in the era of Pius XII's sumptuous monuments. That pontiff, like Mussolini, believed the greatness of the church was tied to the monumental, and they both became involved in lavish buildings.

The place we had settled upon for his meeting with the campesinos was El Roble, a small town centrally located on Guazapa Hill and neighboring Aguacayo, Estanzuelas, Palo Grande, El Zapote, and other communities. We expected a large influx of campesinos and even city people. A nuncio's visit is something very uncommon and important. I explained to the nuncio that we had prepared for a mass in a campesino community and at the end of it he would give his impressions to the faithful and words of inspiration. I also explained to him that the Celebrants of the Word were campesinos who had been prepared to fill that function within the parish.

At that time I had a pickup rather than a car. I asked the nuncio to sit up front, of course, and I had Chus Ángel Bengochea, who was carrying the Communion hosts, sit in back. A few campesinos came with us. We set off for El Roble right away. It was about three in the afternoon. We passed Aguacayo, went through Estanzuelas, and as we got close to the El Roble chapel, three pairs of National Guardsmen came out of the underbrush with their rifle barrels aimed at us. A pair in front kept us from continuing on, and there was a pair on each side of us. One of the Guards, his gun pointed at me, approached and asked me where we were going. Feeling safe at that moment, I told him we were going to El Roble to celebrate a mass. He said, "On orders from above, you cannot continue." I looked at the nuncio and noticed he was pale, trembling from head to toe. I looked behind and Chus Ángel was also pale.

The nuncio tried to say some words in French to me but his voice did not come out. Finally he asked me if the Guards were going to kill us. I told him I did not think so. Then I addressed the Guard: "This man with me, do you know who he is?" He said he did not. I said, "Well, you are violating international law; this man is the Vatican's ambassador to the Salvadoran government. He is protected by agreements to which our country is a signatory, and if anything happens to him, you are going to have a lot of problems, and so is your president. There are many witnesses to what is happening right now."

I saw him hesitate. He did not know what to do. He had probably been sent by the mayor or someone of lower rank. He ordered his Guards to lower their weapons and signaled us to continue. Later Chus Ángel told me, "What a huge scare that was! I almost went in my pants."

We arrived at the chapel and about a thousand people from all the neighboring cantons were there waiting for us. At the end of the service, the nuncio addressed the people with the Word of God and spoke of the importance of nonviolence.

A few days later I visited Monsignor Rivera Damas, who told me the nuncio had received a call from Colonel Molina, who had given him a completely distorted version of what had happened. Apparently, it is easy for a Salvadoran president to lie.

## Chapter 10

# The Cerrón Grande Dam

AMONG THE MOST IMPORTANT events influencing our pastoral work with regard to land was the construction of the Cerrón Grande Dam, along with its companion socioeconomic project. They illustrate the issue of agrarian reform and the need for Suchitoto's campesinos to have better organized themselves. Both the human and technical aspects of the dam's construction merit analysis.

Although it is beyond my expertise to analyze the dam from a technical standpoint, it is really difficult to accept that the solution it provided was the best one, given the country's small size. Even before technical considerations, the question of what development model El Salvador needed in that period undoubtedly should have been asked. This issue is more important than the technical one, and it seems to me the Inter-American Development Bank and the World Bank should have helped come up with a better way to shed light on this question. However, considering both these institutions belong to the prevailing economic system, we can expect little or nothing from them other than the perpetuation of the prevailing system. In actuality, these banks form the pillars on which the system is based, and they care little for the distressing reality our people endure. It seems nobody is interested in the people's fate; to do so is political suicide.

### Announcement of the Construction of the Cerrón Grande Project

On August 14, 1972, Colonel Armando Molina announced the construction of the Cerrón Grande Dam. He did so one and a half months after his inauguration as the country's president, a position to which he was fraudulently elected, a fact he himself admitted to the bishops in one of their regular meetings. On the occasion of the project's announcement, he made the dam's construction contingent on the implementation of a plan to improve the lives of the affected area's inhabitants, who found themselves in a state of true prostration.

The following lines in which he explains why the dam should be built are an extract from the president's speech:[1]

> Ascertainment of the socioeconomic conditions of the locale, characterized by: very high concentration of land tenure and the cultivation of a very small part of the lands, the majority of which are low-yielding; poor productivity of medium and small properties; and the miserable and depressing quality of life of tenant farmers and other agricultural workers, the great majority of whom, as I personally confirmed during my visit to the place, find work opportunities only a few months of the year.
>
> As a result, as the republic's president, I consider that a basic condition to authorizing the dam's construction is the obligation of the executive entity, that is, the Lempa River Executive Commission (CEL), in coordination with other governmental bodies and institutions, as well as the private sector, to be conscious of its responsibilities in this crucial hour of our country's future, to not only cause the least possible economic harm to the zone's inhabitants, but to also carry out a plan allowing for a boost, in a real and effective way, in the levels of well-being of the medium and small farmers and of all the campesinos of Cerrón Grande.
>
> We should publicly recognize the various committees' interest in the human aspects of the problem, and in particular the statement made by the Central American University's 'José Simeón Cañas,' whose concerns have been taken into account.
>
> The plan's fundamental points are the following:
>
> 1. To purchase the land, in cash, at its fair appraised value and to adequately compensate damages or expenses involved in the relocation of agricultural or industrial facilities.
> 2. To facilitate medium-and small-landowners' procurement of lands of equal value nearby, preferably in the same department.
> 3. To organize the campesinos into agricultural cooperatives; to make available to them credit, technical assistance,

---

1. No published records of this speech remain today.

health, education and housing services, and to raise in other ways their standard of living, with the purpose of assuring they have permanent work, and to truly better the living conditions of them and their families.

4. To rebuild homes in Model Communities, as well as all the infrastructure that will be affected.

5. To launch a broad reforestation project in adjoining zones, one that will protect the soils and increase work opportunities.

The government guarantees to all the zone's inhabitants the immediate implementation of this Plan.

At the level of discourse, Molina's proposal appears revolutionary in some of its ideas. It speaks of the region's ailments, which are the same as those of the entire country, that is, the concentration of property ownership in only a few hands, the low percentage of cultivated land, and the "miserable and depressing quality of life of tenant farmers and other agricultural workers."

Clearly, the purpose of making the dam's construction contingent upon an improvement in the quality of life for those affected was to get them on board. However, similar promises have abounded in all previous administrations, meaning that campesinos needed to organize in order to demand those guarantees at the right time. This was the accompaniment work Suchitoto parish was at that moment drawing up, in which area leaders were participating, and in which Father Bernardo Boulang and Father Gregorio Landaverde, assistant to Chalatenango parish, had since joined.

In his first year in office, on July 1, 1972, Molina returned to the subject in his message to the Legislative Assembly. By then there was already strong opposition to the dam's construction by the area's two large landowners, the Bustamantes and the Orellanas, and by some medium-size landowners. What follows is an extract of his speech:

> Upon my arrival in the government, among the major problems to be carefully evaluated was our insufficient supply of electric power, which could put the brakes on short-term possibilities for the country's economic and social progress, especially industrial. . . . I made the decision to authorize the dam's construction provided that the interests of all affected persons were taken into account. For this reason I ordered the creation of the Commission for the Relocation and Comprehensive Development of Cerrón Grande,

whose coordinator—due to the importance I give to the Commission—is the Senior Vice President of the Republic, Dr. Enrique Mayorga Rivas. The instructions I gave the Commission are very clear: with the dam, the inhabitants of Cerrón Grande should live better than they currently live. . . .

The commission to which Molina refers, named on August 15, 1972, was composed of all the ministers of state, including one who subsequently worked very well with the people: Enrique Álvarez Córdova. In addition, it included the president of CEL, Victor de Sola, revered in a special way by the government and private enterprise for his "service to the country."

Building the hydroelectric dam "El Cerrón Grande" (1973)
Photo: Free Images

## The Architect Osegueda

As expected, this brand-new commission was unable to work because it lacked an operational nature. It was a political commission created for demagogic purposes. Therefore, a second special committee of five persons was named, among them: the executive director of CEL; Benjamín S. Valiente, an engineer; and the architect Félix Osegueda Jiménez, the commission's manager. Osegueda studied in Chile during the time of Frei, where he acquired an adequate background in resettling people.

Shortly after opening the commission's regional office in Suchitoto in September 1972, Osegueda paid me a courtesy call. At first glance he seemed to be an easygoing, friendly man, quite self-important, who seriously believed in Molina's political will to fairly benefit the people affected by the dam's construction. I think he had the very good intention of carrying out the relocation project, which he presented as a model of what could be an agrarian reform. During this first visit he outlined his ideas to me, with maps and drawings about his project.

A proposal had been made to establish direct relationships with the affected people, maintaining constant contact with them to fulfill the first goal of making them aware of the objectives of the relocation; in short, the overall improvement of their living standards. The project aimed to create better conditions for the region's campesinos. The project was based on a comprehensive vision of development. It included housing, water, electricity, latrines, schools, clinics, self-government, lands for farming, and the environment. The model was based on Chile's experience with agrarian reform, in which Osegueda participated.

Osegueda had planned a series of courses in different places, including the Monsignor Luis Chávez y González agricultural school. Before year's end, he proposed giving at least twenty courses. The purpose of these courses was not only to inform people about the relocation project, but also to maintain a dialogue with them from which could emerge "decisive conclusions expressed by the communities themselves"—conclusions dealing with housing models acceptable to the campesinos, forms of land tenure and production, health, and so forth.

The planned organizational form was the cooperative. To this end, they would have courses about forming cooperatives and would visit existing cooperatives. In addition and very importantly, within each relocation unit there would be a board of directors, as well as a main board of directors. Participation in these boards was to be democratic. The intention was to have educational elements in the entire relocation process that encouraged citizens to participate in defining the society they wished to establish.

I listened attentively to the architect's presentation and my initial reaction was to support him. I thought it provided a good opportunity to implement some agrarian reform policies, and if the project was truly carried out, the campesinos would benefit. Then and there, however, I shared with Osegueda my doubts as to whether such a project was going to be acceptable to the country's landowners. It would not go unnoticed and soon there would be opposition to it. On the other hand, I told myself, it would have to support the demands for fair land assessments, an immediate concern of those directly affected. The value of their property had to be protected at all costs. After all, it was the only thing they really had and what they could count on for their immediate future; what was offered in return was founded in doubt and subject to many interests.

Architect Osegueda's first visit and his later ones ended up being very useful. They allowed us to become better acquainted with the Relocation Commission's intentions and to plan our activities. From the beginning, our position was not to oppose the dam's construction—we were sure it was a done deal—but rather to get from it the maximum benefit. Even Father Boulang, who had fairly radical outlooks, agreed with us and acted accordingly. Really, the dam issue gave us the chance to advance the political education of the region's campesinos, not only of those directly affected. In fact, many of the campesinos of Guazapa Hill, particularly those from El Zapote, Haciendita, Mirandilla, El Roble, Palo Grande, Estanzuelas, and El Platanar, participated very actively in our meetings at the agricultural school.

The construction of the Cerrón Grande Dam directly affected five municipalities: Suchitoto, Chalatenango, San Luis del Carmen, San Francisco Lempa, and La Toma de Aguilares. Naturally, the effects were different for each town: some were more affected than others. Not all of them lost the same number of inhabitants or the same amount of land, although, according to the plan, the relocated should remain in their own department.

From the outset the commission faced a serious problem. The company contracted to supervise the dam's construction, Harza Engineering of Chicago, did not give much heed to the number affected. According to Harza's census, six thousand people were going to be affected. However, according to a more careful census later made by the commission, this number rose to fifteen thousand people. Of course, the difference was very large, and CEL had no desire to change its relocation budget. According to the engineer Valiente, CEL had not been created to resolve human problems, but rather to produce electrical energy. Very soon this attitude of Valiente's led to clashes between him and Osegueda.

Land, Liberation, and Death Squads

## CEL and the Land Prices

In our meetings about the dam project at the agricultural school, attended by between fifty and two hundred people—attendance varied each month—we encountered two fundamental problems: the price of the lands and the uncertainty experienced by the affected campesinos.

The price of a house can be valued according to the laws of supply and demand, that is, commercially. It can also, however, be valued socially, that is, the value that an individual or a family gives their property because it is their home and community. Family bonds, friendships, and relationships developed through work, religion, pastimes, and political affiliation are very important in individuals' lives. These relationships have an intangible value, much more important in closed societies like those of campesinos. The extended family means a great deal to the rural person. Of course, CEL had no interest in including these considerations in the property assessments of those affected by the dam's construction.

According to CEL, relocated campesinos were going to come out ahead. They would have services they had not had before, such as a market, soccer fields, well-constructed and well-equipped schools, telephones, a post office, and churches, among others. These services cost CEL, a cost that would then have to be deducted from payments for land and homes. However, the campesinos did not see it that way. To begin with, not all were willing to relocate according to the government's project; many families wanted to do it on their own or in family groups.

This divergence of views gave rise to strong friction between those affected and CEL, and, of course, it also impacted the Relocation Commission's plans. The differing viewpoints created quarrels, accusations, protests, and even forced us to organize marches to San Salvador to present lists of demands to the Legislative Assembly. CEL greatly resented the pressure we put on it. The name of Víctor de Sola did not stay so clean, even less so the name of Benjamín Valiente, a materialist for whom the dollar sign was the only thing of interest.

Street in Suchitoto Parish
Photo: Cornell Capa (1972)
International Center of Photography, NY City

## Getting Ourselves Better Organized

Given the situation, we believed monthly meetings were not enough to address the problems of those affected. We had to organize ourselves better; we had to take advantage of the situation before us. From May 1974, we began to give three-day courses to those affected and the region's campesinos at the school of agriculture. We gave a total of ten courses. We dealt with the following three themes: the land was created for everyone and therefore an agrarian reform was necessary; strategies of struggle that would make the relocation a pilot plan of agrarian reform; and how to respond if the relocation was not carried out, namely with a land takeover. Additionally, we sought relationships with campesino associations in the rest of the country and with worker and student organizations. We wanted to get the issue known throughout the nation, as a way to pressure the government and CEL. Our opponents, however, did not care. There would be time to crack down.

This process of awareness-raising, organization, and struggle became the forerunner of the Unified Popular Action Front (FAPU), which was constituted in May 1974 on my initiative. This new initiative is what I call the first FAPU, because a year and a half later it disappeared, to be taken over by National Resistance, later on a member of the FMLN.

## President Molina Visits Some Communities

Little by little and as time went by, the campesinos' feelings heated up. The land assessments were extremely low, much below their commercial price; many of the affected refused to accept them. Given this situation of near despair, in a meeting at the school I dared to suggest we visit Colonel Molina, in order to, as they say, grab the bull by its horns. I imagined the president was little informed of the problems going on in the area, and it seemed advisable to me to inform him of them, especially if at any given moment we were going to have to move to greater struggles in the form of land takeovers.

With the exception of Father Boulang and a couple other priests, the majority accepted my proposal. Clearly it was politically risky; we were giving Molina a chance to look good with the campesinos. However, it seemed to me it was time for the campesinos to meet face-to-face with the country's highest authority to clearly explain to him, without intermediaries, their hopes and worries. This upset many in San Salvador, who defended the strategy of deepening existing divisions. Boulang and Gregorio Landaverde later published a pamphlet in which they did their own analysis of the problems of Cerrón Grande and accused me of playing cat and mouse. They concluded that the cat always eats the mouse. I thought the mouse should learn how to "*torear*,"[2] or provoke, the cat so it knows how to defend itself. In the long run, the practice of always staying in the mousehole, making little secret forays out, does not help much.

I offered to accompany the board members who would visit the president. In fact, I was always present in all their struggles and I would not leave them alone on this occasion. The next day, Monday, I called the president's private secretary, Colonel Velarde Figueroa, a native of San Francisco Lempa, one of the towns that would lose its farmland. He told me he would pass along our request to Molina. In the afternoon the telephone rang; it was the president, who personally confirmed his interest in receiving us on Wednesday. I immediately called together the board and we had a session

---

2. The Spanish verb *torear* describes what a bullfighter does to bait a bull while performing.

to set forth our agenda, our objectives, and a strategy to carry them out. We did not want to go empty-handed.

At the appointed time we arrived at the presidential house. I felt a little nervous, and I imagined that my friends did as well. Those who received us took us to a large, carpeted living room and we waited there for about five minutes. Molina came, accompanied by Osegueda and the director of the National Information Center, Dr. Waldo Chávez. After greetings and mutual introductions, Molina said to us, "Aha, and what brings you here?" His attitude seemed very warm, and this encouraged us to follow our pre-established agenda. Everyone took part, presenting the area's situation and the hopes we had. The president remained silent; he listened attentively to the speakers, who presented the issues of valuations, the need for re-evaluations, relocation, relocation areas, and, especially, demanded respect for the nascent organization of the region's inhabitants.

Before wrapping up, one of the campesinos asked him if he had already heard about the issue presented and he replied that he had not. The same campesino, León Ortega de Copapayo, proposed that he visit us. The president spoke, and agreed to come, without setting a date. That same day, after I had returned to my house very late in the afternoon, Molina called me and told me: "I am going to come visit the area, some four communities, the day after tomorrow. I will come in my helicopter, and I invite you to accompany me." Before ending our telephone conversation, I proposed to him that we visit Copapayo, Santa Teresa, and San Juan. He added El Dorado, inhabited by tenant farmers of the hacienda of the same name. My idea in proposing places was to prepare these communities' leaders, so they would be ready with what they would present.

That very night, Father Boulang accompanied me to Copapayo and we had a meeting with some forty people. The following day I visited Santa Teresa and San Juan; I did not go to El Dorado due to a lack of time. On May 12 I drove my vehicle to an open field on the city's outskirts. I did not tell anyone. As Molina had asked me to do, I gathered branches and made a fire so its smoke would let him know where I was. The helicopter, a French-made Alouette built for civil use, arrived and I climbed aboard. Molina, Osegueda, Waldo, and the pilot were in the helicopter. Waldo had been a member of the Italian Communist Party while he studied at the University of Bologna; however, upon returning to El Salvador, he became entrenched in the government. As he began to enjoy the privileges of power and money, he had become a faithful disciple of Machiavelli. The Salvadoran people know many others who, once professionals, forget their student struggles.

When we arrived in Santa Teresa, the first community on our program, some four hundred people awaited us. Molina felt happy, as did Osegueda. As planned, the leaders immediately took the floor and, with details known only by them, they began to present their problems. Naturally, their major worry was the assessments of their lands. When and how? With what would they be paid? Would they be able to buy something similar to what they were going to lose?

In El Dorado, the community selected by Molina's advisors, the families accused the department commander of Chalatenango, a colonel, and the mayor, of misdeeds. Weeks earlier, the mayor had met with them and told them that since they were tenant farmers, inhabitants of the hacienda, no one had an obligation to pay them for their homes. A CEL official had added that it would only take a matchstick to make them come running from their houses like rats. Many of this community's campesinos could not hide their anger.

On the return to Suchitoto, the colonel made two comments: "I did not know many of these things." And later he angrily referred to the Bustamantes and the Orellanas, rebuking their opposition to the dam's construction and to the country's landowners for their obsession with wealth. I did not know what to think. I had learned to doubt the colonels. In essence, I think, Molina unveiled for me the reality then and now: the army and the president do not rule the country; those who rule the country are the members of the oligarchy.

When I got out of the helicopter, two pairs of Guardsmen came running up. They timidly saluted the president. When I got into my vehicle, I heard a comment from one of them: "These old men pressure us to hate this priest, and look how well they get along with each other."

As a result of this visit, the prices of the lands and houses went up, and the campesinos received better treatment from the assessors and other people who visited them. It gave me the impression that many of the campesinos felt valued again, with new courage to continue their struggle. Molina's visit did not alienate them; on the contrary, it gave them new arguments to demand justice in the relocation. They understood that the project's opposing side was giving weight to their concerns. However, this effect lasted only a very short time.

## Campesinos' Meeting with the Relocation Commission and CEL Personnel

Osegueda, encouraged by Molina's visit to the communities, proposed a meeting with the Relocation Commission and CEL representatives at the agricultural school. Since the campesinos had advanced sufficiently in their understanding of the problems created for them by the relocation, we believed a preparatory meeting was unnecessary. What we did instead was to invite the campesinos of Chalatenango and Suchitoto to participate in this new event.

About four hundred campesinos from the region attended the meeting. Participating on the government's behalf were Dr. Enrique Mayorga Rivas, the country's vice president and coordinator of the Relocation Commission; the engineer Enrique Álvarez Córdova, minister of agriculture; and other representatives, including ministers, secretaries, and advisers. Representing CEL were its president, Victor de Sola; engineer Benjamín Valiente; the executive director; and others. Osegueda was both happy and nervous. I decided to attend, but without speaking. This was to be a dialogue between the campesinos of Cerrón Grande, the government, and CEL.

Many campesinos spoke and received mixed responses. But I remember one who seemed very eloquent and masterful, and for that reason I share here the contribution of Don Francisco Ortiz. He was already on in years, thin, blind in one eye, wearing a hat and sandals and always dressed in white. He said:

> I want to speak to Dr. Mayorga Rivas and to Don Victor de Sola. Doctor Mayorga, I am grateful for what you said about the importance of us campesinos to the country; you are right. I have heard the same thing said on other occasions, for example, in the election campaigns, because you needed our votes. We are important for filling up the ballot boxes, but later, nobody cares about us. You told us on the radio that we were invited to visit anywhere in the country to find land we liked, that it would be ours, because we campesinos of Cerrón Grande are the privileged of this country. We are going to sacrifice our little plots for the dam's construction and we should be rewarded for our sacrifice. You know what we did, Dr. Mayorga? We rented a truck there in my valley of San Juan, on the other side of the Lempa, and some sixty of us went to La Cabaña, to your hacienda, Don Victor.
>
> Don Victor, you have a very beautiful piece of land, all planted in sugarcane. We said this is going to be our land, according to what Dr. Mayorga said. We got to the center of the hacienda,

where your manager came out to see us. We told him: "We come here because these are going to be our lands; we have the government's promise." We explained it to him, and he, alarmed, told us: "Excuse me, gentlemen, but these lands are not for sale." So then, Don Victor, we ought to sacrifice because you need energy, but we cannot have your lands?

Don Victor, you are a very intelligent and well-educated man, as are all who have come to visit us. But I think, and I am an unschooled man, that you all made a mistake, because it seems to me that you failed to do three studies. You had to first see whether flooding these lands was necessary or if something else could be done. You had to think about our fate, the fate of thousands of us, because we as people are more important than a dam. And finally, did you all stop to think about the consequences of this dam? Once the waters rise, millions of mosquitoes and other insects will emerge, and who are they going to bite? You who live far away, or us campesinos? But you did not do these studies, because the only thing that interests you is to have more energy for your factories.

Later I found myself with Enrique Álvarez Córdova, president of the Democratic Revolutionary Front (FDR), in Washington, DC, and I reminded him of this memorable meeting. He commented that he had never seen Enrique Mayorga more furious than on that occasion, and for the first time had seen tears roll from Don Víctor's eyes. The old man cried from anger and shame.

Indeed there were many changes after this meeting. Osegueda felt he had to step down from his position, despite Molina's interest in keeping him on. Benjamín Valiente became tougher and more insufferable. According to him, going around in all these circles was not necessary to build a few houses for poor campesinos; a mason could build them without so much song and dance. The project as Osegueda had designed it had failed, and with it, all its benefits evaporated. It is true that the architect had made mistakes, but they were due in part to the lack of collaboration between CEL and the government. Since then, Valiente's right-hand man, the engineer Guandique, had planned a new relocation project, which did not take into account those to be affected. Many rejected it and solved their problems on their own; others, having no choice, accepted it.

Meanwhile, the principals involved continued to assess and re-assess houses and lands. In our monthly meetings at the agricultural school, the campesinos of Santa Bárbara, department of Cabañas, and their neighbors in Copapayo, in Suchitoto's jurisdiction, gave alarming news about the appraisals.

No one trusted the government or CEL. This forced us to plan some actions to denounce what was going on; among other things, we decided to march to the Legislative Assembly to ask the representatives for protection.

The opposition legislators demanded that a commission consisting of the area's congressional representatives be named. The Assembly president rejected the idea, which was fair, and asked the Commission of Social Welfare to take care of the problem. The commission did nothing. The campesinos immediately realized that very little could be accomplished at this level.

The social value of the properties was not taken into account, nor even the regional market value. Some were paid twice, others received a fair price, the majority less than market price, and a few did not receive anything because they had lost their deeds. There was someone who was imprisoned for having received double payment and having spent it. The disarray and injustice of the matter became apparent. The expert assessors visited the communities Saturdays and Sundays, bringing ice chests in their vehicles to keep their beers nice and cold or to mix hard drinks along the way. Depending on the alcohol's proof, sometimes they correctly measured the lots and other times they took wild guesses, because "good" they were not.

## Relocation of the Campesinos

Approximately eleven hundred families were relocated to the area north of the dam. To the south, in Suchitoto, the government built a small housing project in Copapayo. That was the way in which Suchitoto's campesinos and I were punished for our actions in opposing the government plans.

Our objective in the final stage was to support the relocations. We insisted that each lot on which a campesino family's little house would be built should have a minimum of seven hundred square yards, to maintain the campesinos' idea of adequate housing space. The CEL decided on smaller lots. Engineers Valiente and Guandique arranged for housing construction in a flat area, one with clay soil and no drainage that becomes muddy during rainy season.

They built septic tanks one-meter deep for two or three families' use. The foul smell nauseated the shacks' inhabitants. The excessive humidity, dammed-up water, and the mud and filth unleashed a tremendous plague of mosquitoes. Malaria appeared and the families watched their children and elderly, especially, die of it. The malaria problem was even worse in the cantons neighboring the dam, where they received no attention. The plague of mosquitoes was intolerable in Los Palitos and in Copapayo. At sundown, the children began to cry because they could not stand the insect bites and the incessant buzz in their ears. In their distress, people gathered cow manure and burnt it at night to produce smoke to drive away the mosquitoes. But this was worse because, due to the lack of oxygen, they suffered nausea and dizziness.

For the first time in a long time, the communities faced three types of mosquitoes: Culex, Anopheles, and another that transmits falciparum. The illness transmitted by this last one is fatal. To try to help the campesinos in this new situation they faced, I visited the Department of Public Health, where technicians told me that controlling this pestilence meant an investment of approximately one million two hundred thousand colones, and they did not have it.

Because the homes' courtyards were so small, those who owned a mule and cow tied them up to the hallway's pillars. Pigs, chickens, and dogs lived alongside children. Clearly, although the houses looked nicer and had electricity and water, the campesinos were not happy; they felt displaced, out of their element. Moreover, entrance gates were installed at the housing project; the gates closed at six in the evening and opened at five in the morning. Because of this, the inhabitants said they lived in concentration camps. Some left. It was evident that the situation constituted a time bomb.

## People Not Relocated and Eduardo Orellana's Death

A good number of people remained outside the relocation projects. They did so either by choice—finding ways to move on their own—or because they were not eligible according to CEL rules. Among others, for example, were the tenant farmers of the Colima hacienda, which is in Suchitoto's jurisdiction and Aguilares parish. The Orellana brothers, owners of Colima, had received only a percentage of the lands' value; they would be paid the rest in twenty-year-term bonds. Many tenant families lived on the haciendas; upon finding themselves homeless, they had demanded that CEL relocate them, without receiving any reply. These families accused the Orellanas of negligence for not interceding in their case. The families were affected by the dam, which damaged their sources of potable water. On December 5, some two hundred campesinos asked for an audience with the Orellanas to present their complaints and demands. Among the demands, they had planned to ask the Orellanas for land in the non-flooded portion to build their small houses.

The Orellana brothers refused to receive them, and the campesinos, after staging a rally, decided to leave. At that moment, brothers Francisco and Eduardo Orellana came out armed with revolvers and fired, reportedly into the air, intending to intimidate the tenant farmers, the very people who had contributed, year after year, to the accumulation of the Orellanas' riches. According to the campesinos' version, while they were firing, Francisco accidentally injured his brother Eduardo, and he died half an hour later. As expected, Francisco accused the campesinos of his brother's death. The truth is that if one of them had been the killer, he would have been immediately arrested, because there were four police officers and a captain there, carrying G3s, rifles, which the campesinos feared.

The Orellana brothers belonged to the Eastern Region Farmers Front (FARO), an organization founded mainly by cotton and sugarcane growers in 1974 to impede Molina's planned agrarian reform. FARO was formed by a significant number of landowners opposing the Catholic Church, because the church was dedicated to raising campesinos' consciousness in various regions. In Aguilares the Jesuit fathers carried out very valuable work with the campesinos. In Suchitoto the campesinos were organized. FECCAS, the Federation of Christian Campesinos, also operated in this region and had carried out various protest activities. A group of families from Los Palitos asked me if I could help them with relocation and with them my parish team formed a cooperative, of which I will write later. FARO immediately launched accusations against FECCAS, the Jesuits, and the area's parishes. They accused us of being communists, murderers, of subverting the public order and fighting to take over power.

The Cerrón Grande constituted for many of us a first-class experience that allowed us to evaluate our strengths and weaknesses. Although we wanted to present a common front, we did not always have unified leadership. Sometimes the differences were felt, for example, in how we should deal with the government and CEL. While I was more interested in finding a suitable solution to the campesinos' upcoming dilemma, Father Boulang maintained a longer-term position oriented to the country's needed structural changes. However, this experience allowed us to delve deeper into the issue of agrarian reform, to experience the land problem in all its rawness, to improve in campesino organization, and to learn firsthand the limitations of governmental and institutional endeavors, as well as those of private enterprise, to solve the problems of the needy. We learned that they were the problem, and that we should look for other means to advance the cause of the poorest.

## Chapter 11

# 1974 Elections

## A Warrant is Issued for the Alas Priests' Arrest for Their Anarchic Attitudes

### Elections of Mayors and Representatives

THE BEGINNING OF 1974, an election year for mayors and legislative representatives throughout the country. Once again, political passions have ignited in the "Tom Thumb of America." Elections in El Salvador have a cathartic function. They represent a kind of emotional escape from the political order's repression, an outlet for people who lack the power of self-determination. The majority does not decide, votes do not count, they have already been counted ahead of time. Electoral fraud has been an essential part of the democracy prescribed by the leaders of the oligarchy and military. No one panics; within the oligarchy there has been an elite leadership, led for many years by Miguel Dueñas, which decides the nation's fate. Evidently, this is a lesser evil than communism in the innocent eyes of the US ambassador. Why worry about small matters, he thinks, if El Salvador is but a small piece of the North American backyard?

In Suchitoto's political struggle, in essence two parties participated. These were the National Conciliation Party (PCN), founded by the military in 1961, and the Christian Democratic Party (PDC). The way in which elections were carried out make them seem more like a cockfight or a bullfight: someone must come out dead or at least badly wounded. Accusations abound on both sides. Slander is the order of the day, clothed in anonymity.

## 1974 ELECTIONS

This is a very valuable tool available to PCN followers, aimed at discrediting their perceived political enemies.

## Defamations

During the election season, it was very common for one to get up in the morning and open the door of one's house to find a leaflet full of false accusations. Under the shadow of night, sheltered by darkness, some demon went around the city strewing these flyers, leaving them in crevices of windows and doors. The tactic of discrediting others plays a very important role. In my case, there was much interest in isolating me from those in the city who supported me, the majority affiliated with the PDC. Thus, the defamers tried to mix our support of struggles for justice with party politics. In their desire to harm others, they did not care if they stained the names of honorable people in our society. Their depravity had no limits; if it was necessary to accuse women known for their rectitude of indecent acts, so be it.

Not a few but several times I found these handbills at six in the morning when I went to celebrate mass. Sometimes the sacristan had picked them up because they left them on the church pulpit, supposedly to provoke my anger. As can be imagined, these flyers made me very sad; I thought of the people whose very personal honor was called into question. However, the struggle I had accepted on behalf of campesinos' rights helped me rise above it. My knowledge of cultural anthropology also helped me understand those who accused me. My studies in Ecuador about the values held by each strata of society, of the radicalized, of the oppressed, of the dependent, and of the oppressors, allowed me to understand the different behaviors of individuals and of groups. However, that does not mean I justified them, much less accepted them.

If one understands the reasons why someone acts in one way or another, one is already halfway to understanding their attitudes and ways of acting. Moreover, these people were protected by those in higher positions in San Salvador. Smear tactics already had a history in Latin America. All one has to do is recall the well-known Banzer Plan, named after the Bolivian ex-president, inspired by the CIA to fight the supposedly subversive clergy. The plan had the following tenets:

1. Never attack the church as an institution, let alone the bishops as a group. Rather, attack that part of the church known as "progressive."

2. Mainly attack the foreign clergy. Continually insist they are preaching armed warfare and that they are connected with international communism and have been sent to this country for the sole purpose of dragging the church toward communism.

3. Control some religious orders.

4. The CIA has decided to directly take part in this matter. It has promised to give us information about some priests (personal documents, studies, friends, addresses, publications, and contacts abroad).

5. Control some religious houses.

6. For the moment, do not repress any religious houses because doing so will cause much controversy.

7. Confront the hierarchy with *fait accompli*.

8. Arrests should be made in the countryside, on solitary streets, or late at night. Once the priest has been arrested, the agent should leave subversive material in his briefcase and, if possible, in his room or house, and a gun, preferably a large-caliber pistol. Have a story prepared to discredit him in the eyes of his bishop and the public.

9. Using any means of communication, publish licentious, bold, compromising material to discredit priests and members of religious orders who represent progressive elements in the church. Ask for an official signature on any statement so we may know where it is from and who wrote it.

10. Maintain a friendly relationship with some bishops, with some members of the church, and some native priests. That way we ensure that public opinion does not believe there is systematic persecution of the church, but only a few of its dissident members. Insist on the authenticity of the national church (as opposed to the church in other countries).

11. Reward agents who best carry out this action plan, giving them belongings confiscated from the homes of priests and members of religious orders.

This plan was known and applied in the entire continent. Of that we were all sure. The National Information Center of the Presidential House dealt with its wide dissemination and practice. In El Salvador the plan was aimed not only against Jesuits and other religious orders who devoted themselves to ministry with the most humble, but also to some fifty of us diocesan priests at the forefront of pastoral service to the people. Suchitoto could not escape this persecution.

The names of mayor Mario Rivera Monterrosa, of ex-mayor Guadrón, of Alfredo Mata, of Pepe Rivera, of Tapón Manuel Dubón, and several others were among the main slanderers of our work and of us as individuals. My brother suffered, Bernardo suffered, the campesinos suffered, we all suffered the onslaught of these demons of slander and lies. Still today, after so many years, my heart cries as I write these lines. Democracy cannot be born of lies. Violence is born of deceit, and that is what El Salvador will reap abundantly.

## Election Day

Storm clouds darkened election day. The political environment in the countryside and city was charged with conflicting energies. We all expected violence. PCN managers had asked village prostitutes and the most aggressive market women to dress in white and blue, the flag's colors. A well-known store in town had donated fabric for their dresses. A landowner offered to pay them five colones for the day. Someone else had given them knives. In this election, the PCN would not directly use the National Guard to brutally repress the opposition; this time, the task would be done by the city's poorest people, by the prostitutes, by those who for pennies were filled with hate and illicit power.

On the eve of the March election day, the city filled with opposition campesino leaders who had agreed to take care of the ballot boxes during voting hours, for which they had to have advance meetings. Others were there because they wanted to vote early, before something happened. Starting early that Sunday, the candidates and party leaders scurried about. They came and went from one voting place to another. Certainly they were not participating in a celebration of democracy and voting power, but rather in a political passion, power for power's sake. They therefore looked nervous, their face muscles tense, like hunted animals.

Voting began at seven in the morning. The lines were long, formed mostly of opposition members who wanted to vote early so as not to lose the first hours that are relatively free of interference. At eight o'clock the women dressed in white and blue appeared. Each looked like an Amazon. With knives in hand they first began to threaten recognized opposition politicians, and then the campesinos, merely for being campesinos. The women acted like hardened San Quintin criminals. A short distance behind the women were twelve National Guardsmen armed with G3s, the dreadful German-made automatic rifles. Thinking there may be a massacre, those in line to vote disbanded; they fled, pursued by the women dressed in white and blue.

At nine in the morning, the city returned to calm. The polls had been closed. The people returned home. The democratic celebration, PCN style, had ended. The only thing left to do was declare Mario "Prud" of the PCN the winning candidate, which was done at five o'clock that afternoon to comply with the rules.

## The Alas Priests Incite Rebellion

Mario had won the mayorship. But he had unfinished business on behalf of the Presidential House: to kick the Alas brothers out of Suchitoto. For this he had resort to new defamation: to accuse the Alas priests of inciting the campesinos to revolt.

During the months of July and August 1974, the most sensationalist and scandal-mongering news in all the newspapers was the accusation that we were sponsoring a campesino rebellion so we could take power. The news was ridiculous, but it was accepted by our famous free press, *El Diario de Hoy* and the *Prensa Gráfica*. For more than a month prior to these slanders, Mario "Prud"—a nickname our people gave the mayor due to the ease with which he switched from the PRUD to the PCN, both parties founded by the military—had begun a well-orchestrated campaign from San Salvador against us. Mario had funds from the Presidential House, directly from Waldo Chávez Velasco's[1] office, and the support of his party's most radical members, mostly market people and some landowners, to carry out his accusation. Their goal was to get us out of Suchitoto. In statements to the national media, they used the most well-known epithets of anti-clerical jargon and cheap politics, such as "wolves in sheepskin," "communists," and others.

For two months the PCN organized protests in San Salvador. They staged these in front of the San José de la Montaña seminary, where the archdiocesan offices were located, in front of the newspaper buildings, and sometimes in front of the Presidential House. The demonstrations culminated in a rally at which speakers took turns demanding the "removal of the priests of Suchitoto." Each time there was a protest, the news appeared in all the papers with photos showing an amazing number of banners. Some

---

1. Waldo Chávez Velasco was a journalist and leading public intellectual of the PCN.

read as follows: "False priests, get out of our humble and religious town of Suchitoto"; "Canton Caulote says: we no longer want the Alas priests or their communism in Suchitoto"; "Mr. President, we beg you to use your influence to get the subversive Alas priests transferred"; "Suchitoto women, for the love of God, demand the removal of the Alas priests"; "the citizens of Suchitoto hate violence and terror, we ask for the transfer of Inocencio and Higinio," and so on.

Besides the demonstrations in San Salvador, they also organized others in Suchitoto in front of our house very early in the morning or at nightfall. The slogans they shouted at us were always the same. Their intent was to intimidate us, to destroy our nerves, make us flee the city. Alfredo Mata, an unemployed man, always led the demonstrations. It seemed that in the past he had a lot of money, but he spent it all and ended up in the service of the town's politicians, who were rewarding him with a few cents.

It was a tragicomic situation. Tragic because it could end in violence, imprisonment, or in our departure from Suchitoto for good; comic because the idea of the campesinos rising up to attempt a coup was out of all proportion to their means, nor could it be done within a parish's structure. When it came to politics, however, anything could be said and asserted. All one needed was an imagination and a sick mind. Besides, the newspapers would readily print anything if it was for the benefit of the class they represented.

In the face of the mayor's accusations, published in the newspapers, we of course responded through the press. I share here one of our replies, because it provides information about the atmosphere prevailing in Suchitoto at that time. It is in response to Mario asking the Interior Ministry to investigate our activities. The reply, dated August 11, 1974, reads:

> We are responding to the accusations that Suchitoto's mayor makes against us, the two priests, brothers José Inocencio Alas and Higinio Alas, not due to the accuser's prominence, but to clarify things in all honesty.
>
> 1. I continue being parish priest of Suchitoto. It is false that I have been removed. His Excellency Monsignor Luis Chávez can testify to this.
> 2. I am not secretary of the archbishop's "palace," but rather executive secretary of pastoral work.
> 3. I do not insult the authorities:
>    - I respect those who have been legitimately elected leaders by the Salvadoran people.

- I respect the president of the republic. I have conversed at length with him; he knows my intentions, as I know his way of thinking. I admire him for many things, which does not mean I do not criticize him for other things, just as he can also criticize me. Constructive criticism allows individuals and societies to grow; it is the base of true democracy. We are enriched by one another's thinking in finding solutions to the problems we face.

- Yes, I have criticized, and I continue to criticize, the standstill of the announced agrarian reform, the glacial pace of the relocation of the campesinos affected by the construction of the Cerrón Grande Dam, etc. This does not mean I call our president an assassin.

4. I have not called Suchitoto's rich "bloodsuckers," first, because to generalize is false; second, because there are some admirable landowners in the city. Yes, I must, and yes, I have denounced injustices that some of them commit against campesinos. There are still some people in the area who in sugarcane season pay one colón for the work. You can verify this with the Ministry of Labor. Also there are those who pay ten colones. I never call myself anyone's advocate. I work so all individuals may discover their capacity to become adults, not in order to advocate for anyone.

5. Yes, my brother and I denounce the murder of Emilio Acosta, a campesino from Canton Trinidad, killed by a municipal police officer in front of many witnesses. The case is currently being sorted out in the city's district court. Witnesses have stated that the campesino was not armed. There were not ten, but four, campesinos who were returning to their homes. They were drunk but not offending anyone. The police wanted to arrest and jail them so they would have to pay the respective fine. The incident is not unusual. This is how it goes in Suchitoto. They bring in groups of people in the garbage truck, especially on Saturdays and Sundays. The truck makes several trips. They even take some people off their horses, whether or not the individuals are drunk, and they fine them *and* their horse, up to a *colón*. At city hall they torture them. Cases: Ángel Roberto Acosta, Oscar Monge, Porfirio Casco, and the friends of the murdered man, a brother, and a minor

whom they seized, demanding that they declare they had provoked the police officers, and so on and so forth.

Additionally in Suchitoto, the mayor, arrogating rights belonging to the honorable Legislative Assembly, eight days after taking office proclaims martial law: neither adults nor young people can walk the streets after nine-thirty at night. The president of the Legislative Assembly can verify this fact.

6. It is true that a rally had been called on a Sunday. It is not true:

- That we priests organized it.
- That we are in favor of the use of weapons. On the contrary, we believe a tractor is worth more than a tank, a cow is more valuable than a pistol.
- We have never spoken of burning stores. What for? Nor city hall. Yes, we hope someday it will stop being a place of torture and will become the people's house, as it was in the days of Beto López, the ex-mayor of the PCN.
- Acts of terrorism make no sense, because the only thing we would achieve is tremendous repression; and besides, the Sacas' store or the burning of the municipal building, what do they mean, countrywide? Does the mayor believe that in killing the flea we have killed the dog?
- Yes, we lament the Guards' coming to Suchitoto. He is tiring them out for nothing. They are people and should not be at the service of a sick man.

7. We are not the ones who provoke hatred, terror, division, but rather he, who to get himself elected mayor, beat a person guarding the ballot boxes. He paid women to wear uniforms and attack with knives. He personally tortures prisoners in city hall; he holds a pistol to Porfilio Casco's chest, telling him he is going to be the second victim he is going to kill, and so on.

# Land, Liberation, and Death Squads

Demonstration in San Salvador against the Alas priests
Photo: Diario de Hoy (1974)

## Judge Orders the Arrest of the Alas Brothers

Due to the accusations of Mario Prud and his town councilmen, the Interior Minister, Colonel Agustín Martínez Varela, instructed the governor of Cuscatlán, under whose jurisdiction we fell, to investigate the truthfulness of the accusations. However, as the *Diario Latino* had reported, "The Ministry has been very discreet and thoughtful about this particular issue, which seems more like small-town personal-political gossip than a case of special importance meriting the attention of higher authorities." The night before ordering our arrest, the judge came to my house with Omar Alas, who was in charge of our case, and with little ado said, "I will have to issue a warrant to have you both arrested during the time of the inquiry into the charge made against you. Because it seems to me everything is false, that Mario is obeying orders from above, I am going to communicate beforehand through Omar the day I do it. Find a nice place to retreat for a few days."

The following day I needed to go to San Salvador on personal business. I left my house around ten in the morning and as I approached San Rafael La Bermuda, I saw in the rearview mirror that somebody was following me at high speed. He passed me and signaled me to stop. Right away, I recognized Omar and I obeyed his signal. All in a hurry, he told me: "Do not come back.

Gómez Zárate has delivered the warrant to the Guard and they are going to begin looking for you throughout the entire country. Since the Guard wants you, they are going to do everything possible to catch you. I have already advised your brother Higinio, and he has left by way of Aguilares." I thanked him, and I went as quickly as possible to San Salvador.

I obviously could not stay with relatives as the security forces would easily find me in such places. I thought of my old friends from the cursillos de Cristiandad and I could come up with no better person than Toño Díaz, owner of Publicidad Díaz. He was a bachelor, happy, a kind and faithful friend. I called him from a public telephone and without hesitation he said he would be honored to have me stay at his house. That was Toño Díaz. He called the archbishop to let him know I was in a safe place, with all the comforts of home, including a backyard swimming pool. There I spent two weeks reading and resting. I avoided phone calls so I did not fall into some trap. In El Salvador the telephones of the opposition were monitored, and Antonio (Toño) was a Christian Democrat. I worried about my brother's whereabouts, because I did not know where he was. Once I was free, he told me he stayed in the Colonia Escalón with some of his friends.

## Molina Will Make a Statement in the Case of the Alas Priests

Our arrest warrant was announced widely. Having already been published by other newspapers days before, the *Diario Latino* ran a story later in the week that read as follows:

> Yesterday the Third Criminal Court received the warrant from the judge of the Court of First Instance of Suchitoto, Dr. Antonio Augusto Gómez Zárate, in which he asks the President of the Republic, Colonel Arturo Armando Molina, to make a statement against the offenders in the ongoing case against the priests José Inocencio and Higinio Alas, charged with the crime of "instigating rebellion."
>
> The aforementioned request mentions the statement of the witness Adrián Lara Guadrón, in which he comments that in the month of April of the current year, he heard during a mass at which Father José Inocencio Alas officiated that campesinos should rise up in arms against the government to end the misery in which the people live.

This news created problems for Molina, forcing him to seek advice. He had confidence in Father Roberto Trejos and consulted him. Once we were free, Trejos told me that Molina called him and asked his opinion about the statement he was requested to make. Trejos told him: "It is best to make no statement, for the following reasons: if you make a statement against the Alas priests, the army and the rich are going to be happy and the Church will be upset; if you make a statement in favor of the Alas priests, the Church will be happy, but the army and the rich will be upset. The best thing is to make no statement." Molina followed his advice and made no statement.

A few days after the papers wrote of the warrant's being issued, on August 28, the *Diario de Hoy* published breaking news. The charges against my brother were dismissed due to a request presented to the judge by Omar Alas. However, according to the *Prensa Gráfica* of August 29, I was denied dismissal of charges because there was sufficient evidence against me of "inciting people to rebel against the current government and preaching anarchy and anti-democratic doctrines." Later, on September 7, the judge declared me free of all charges of which I'm accused, allowing me to get back to work without the risk of being arrested.

Suchitoto parishioners signal V for victory as they await the return of the Alas brothers
Photo: Diario de Hoy (1974)

## Detained by the Police

Days before my brother was declared free of all charges, Omar Alas had asked for my release with bail, which the judge had accepted. This allowed me to return to my town, although the case continued. I planned my return for August 24. I met with Monsignor Chávez and told him I was determined to continue my work in the same place, even if it meant having to face a host of dangers.

Monsignor Chávez saw fit to have someone with enough weight in government circles to accompany me. He told me he would ask this favor of Monsignor Óscar Romero, his assistant bishop. Monsignor Chávez was not happy with the performance of his assistant, who avoided responsibility, participated very little in clergy meetings, and easily took refuge in the homes of the rich. Monsignor said to me: "This way he will have to be exposed a little to public opinion. He has to engage more with us."

I had known Monsignor Romero since 1962 when, as priest of the Calvario parish in San Miguel, he participated in a cursillo de Cristiandad I directed. From then on, we began a friendship, even though we were ideologically poles apart. I was pleased he would accompany me. At three in the afternoon on Saturday, August 24, we left for Suchitoto. We had planned the mass of thanksgiving for our return at five that afternoon, to give ourselves enough time.

We went, just the two of us, Monsignor Romero and I. My brother was already in the parish. Monsignor drove and I rode next to him. On the outskirts of San Bartolomé Perulapía, we saw a National Police patrol car. They signaled us to stop and Monsignor obeyed their orders, although he became a bit nervous. He mumbled a question to himself: "And what do they want?"

As usual, they asked for his license and the vehicle's registration card. They examined the documents and asked us to get out of the car, because they wanted to inspect it. They clearly wanted to cause us trouble. Monsignor opened the car's trunk and they went through my bag. At the bottom I kept a simple .22-caliber pistol. They asked Monsignor about the weapon and he said it belonged to him. Since it was obvious the bag did not belong to him, I told them: "It is actually mine. I have an agricultural school in Suchitoto where there are cattle. When the cows give birth, *chuchos* (dogs) come to eat the placenta and there is danger of the chuchos killing the calf." Monsignor realized my insistence in mentioning the word "chucho," because that is a local slang term for police officers.

As a result of their search, they ordered us to return to the Pan-American Highway and go to Cojutepeque. When we arrived in that city, Monsignor told the police chief about the mission entrusted to him by Monsignor Chávez and how he was his auxiliary bishop. The chief replied that he only obeyed the orders of his superiors and told us to take a seat. Monsignor asked for the telephone to call the president of the republic.

He was very annoyed and felt humiliated in his dignity as bishop. Reluctantly they handed him the device and he called the Presidential House. Molina was not in his office, so he called Molina's private residence. As he was unable to speak directly with the President, he told the person who answered what was happening. After about half an hour the phone rang, the police officer answered the call, and when he was done speaking, he came to us and told us we could leave.

## V for Victory

We thought that nobody would be waiting for us in Suchitoto now. We had lost almost two hours, which meant we would arrive late for mass. A few blocks before reaching the edge of town, we saw a lot of people in the street who began shouting our names and making the "V for victory" sign. Some shot off fireworks from their home courtyards. At the entrance to town we were met by a large crowd that had been waiting there for us for more than three hours, even though more than thirty National Guardsmen had been threatening them, pointing their rifle barrels at them. All that time, the people had been praying, shouting slogans, singing the national anthem and church songs, and waiting for us. According to the *Diario de Hoy*, which was never in favor of our work, "about fifteen thousand people" had gathered "to cheer the priests José Inocencio and Higinio Alas, returning to the city after being exonerated of charges of inciting the people."

In front of that crowd, at the very front, there was a woman, happy and proud of what she was experiencing and feeling. Her face was adorned with a beautiful smile. She had stayed with the people the entire time, willing to take all possible risks. She was my mother, the woman who inspired me each moment of my life and who nurtured my courage in the most difficult times. At her side was my brother Sabino, who has never left me alone, and Higinio, my partner in work and success.

From the entrance, arms raised and our fingers signaling V for victory, we headed to the park in front of the church. The crowd was too large to think about celebrating the Eucharist within its walls. Monsignor Romero presided over the mass and gave the sermon. In spite of being a very conservative man, during his sermon he analyzed our national reality and invited the people to continue fighting for justice, peace, and liberty.

*Chapter 12*

# The Unified Popular Action Front

## Context

THE IDEA OF CREATING a mass movement does not arise spontaneously. In Suchitoto it resulted from a process that had been emerging for some time, having as its starting point evangelization born of our commitment to the community and our faith. If we ask Jesus what his commitment is, what mission the Father entrusted in him, his answer is clear; we recorded it at the beginning of this book and we repeat it here, like the leitmotif of a symphony. I think this is necessary because, certainly, by the Father's sending Jesus to set up his tent among us, he did so in obedience to a plan he had established for his Son and for us. God is the least spontaneous of all beings.

Jesus said:

> The Spirit of the Lord is on me,
> because he has anointed me
> to proclaim good news to the poor.
> He has sent me to proclaim freedom for the prisoners
> and recovery of sight for the blind,
> to set the oppressed free,
> to proclaim the year of the Lord's favor.
>
> Today this scripture is fulfilled in your hearing.[1]

---

1. Luke 4:18–19 and 21b, NIV.

A parish's pastoral work should be based on the ministry Jesus developed with the people of Israel. Pastoral work obeys the Christian mission and commitment. The transmission of that mission and commitment is evangelization. In Suchitoto, this process, which never ends, lasted three long years in its most intensive phase. At the same time, due to the needs arising from Suchitoto's historical reality, we had to include in the work, as an essential element, our responses to existing social problems; that is, a social ministry.

In the name of his mission, a pastor cannot refuse to get involved in the "worries and hopes" of his people, as Vatican II concluded in the beginning of *Gaudium et Spes*. The refusal to do so means any of these three things: to disregard theology, which often happens; to prefer to live a comfortable life; or to be afraid. In any of these three situations, the pastor should do something else and not be a pastor. Given El Salvador's existing economic, political, and social structure, which were beholden to the interests of the oligarchy, the army, and the American Embassy, our clamor for the people's rights was not heard, forcing us to usher in a new stage in our work with the campesinos. This new stage was their participation in the political arena, a right they have for the simple reason of being people, belonging to a society and a nation. Participation in the political arena started almost from the beginning, but did not consolidate until the creation of the Unified Popular Action Front (FAPU), a mass movement created to demand rights, which later evolved into politics.

## Origin of the Idea of FAPU

In March 1974 we had countrywide elections for representatives and mayors. The next month, as usual, the Celebrants of the Word and I had our regular meeting, which lasted all night Saturday into Sunday morning. As always, after the prayer we began by analyzing the reality of those days. On that occasion, our attention centered on the recent elections. We needed to evaluate them and work out the consequences for the country and the campesinos. From our analysis we concluded things would continue exactly the same, with the same dependence and the same oppression. What could we hope for from representatives and mayors elected through fraud? Would the representatives and mayors perhaps have some power in the country? What independence exists among the state's three powers? We concluded that the answer to each of these was the same: none.

With these considerations, I proposed we better organize ourselves before the new legislative assembly and our mayor, Mario Rivera, took office. I proposed we enter into negotiations with ANDES, the two then-existing universities, and the associations of workers and campesinos. It was about establishing an alliance for defending the people's rights. My idea was well-received among the group of campesinos, and we immediately organized ourselves into commissions to go visit our future companions in the struggle.

We planned to first visit Mario López, secretary-general of the National Association of Teachers (ANDES), and Mélida Anaya Montes, Mario's colleague in the organization. We had an excellent relationship with Mario due to the support we gave ANDES during the second teachers' strike. As expected, Mario and Mélida gave our proposal a very warm welcome, eager to form a common front in our struggles. We consulted with them about next steps, and they told us which colleagues we should visit among the workers and students.

We held our first meetings in Suchitoto. The teachers, some students, and Celebrants of the Word participated. However, we feared security agents were watching us, and at the end of May we decided to move our meetings to San Salvador, where our presence could pass unnoticed. Of course, we were committed to starting in a big way, with the larger assistance from those interested in our project.

**Wake for a FAPU member killed by National Guardsmen (1975)**
**Photo: Free Images**

## FAPU's Foundation

We asked ourselves where to hold our first session in the capital, and I proposed the Sacred Heart Basilica. It had a meeting room built during my time with the cursillos de Cristiandad, which was very spacious and airy, able to hold some four hundred people. I offered to speak with the parish priest, Father Cortés, to see if he would allow us use it. Father Cortés is a friendly man, simple, dedicated to his work. He asked me who would participate in the meetings and, smiling, requested that I not get him into trouble.

At least two hundred participants attended this meeting, among them campesinos, teachers, students, and workers. I introduced the idea, which Mario then amplified, and discussion began on our objectives, the activities we hoped to carry out, and the organizational structure needed to do so. For me it was all a surprise. It was clear I was in an environment I was not used to, a much more political environment of endless ideological discussions. It was during this meeting that we gave our project a name. A student from the National University proposed we name it the Popular Unified Action Front (FAPU). The title was put to a vote and approved, because it best represented the objectives we had adopted.

## Organizational Structure

We structured FAPU around the participant organizations. During the first months, at least three campesino organizations participated; on behalf of workers there was FUSS; there were at least three student groups; and on teachers' behalf was ANDES. There was also representation of the clergy who are most committed to their parishes' destinies. Each organization enjoyed voting rights, although it was agreed to decide matters through mutual consensus.

From the outset we perceived tensions among the different organizations. Behind the tensions lay the forefront of what would later, in early 1980, become the FMLN. Each group tried to work things to its own advantage, causing ideological friction among the parts. A central committee was formed of representatives of the organizations; it met very frequently in different places in the center of the country. We especially liked to meet in the parish convent of Father Cayo Ayala in Cojutupeque and also in the house of some women religious in San Antonio Abad.

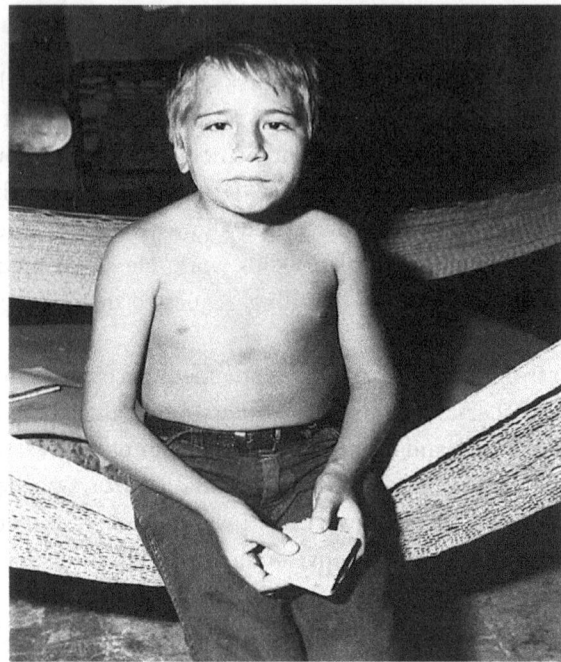

A boy eating a sandwich in his hammock
Photo: Rick Reinhard

## FAPU's Dissolution

FAPU was the first attempt at mass organization. Although it had its virtues and served the country's revolutionary cause, it did not achieve its objective due to the left's tendency to *caciquismo*,[2] an evil embedded in our people's cultural roots. Each leader believed his ideological position was most in line with the country's historical reality, that his analysis was most appropriate to solving its problems, and that he should be at the head and the others must follow. Those who were most articulate won these debates and they became entrenched in their positions as *caciques*. Death alone had the power to remove them.

To corroborate this assertion about the inclination to caciquismo, it suffices to recall what happened during some demonstrations held in Suchitoto by followers of the National Resistance and the FPL. They treated each other spitefully; each group destroyed the literature the other had

---

2. *Caciquismo*, based on the word *cacique*, or chieftain, connotes tyrannical leadership, usually by a single person or "boss."

distributed to the public. I asked myself whether the revolution's number one enemy was the oligarchy, the military, or the left's lack of unity.

We experienced the same worm of disunity in FAPU. It was clear some had joined in order to achieve a position of strength or to gain an advantage. This led us to ask some of them to leave FAPU, as in the case of the two worker representatives of FUSS; others left by choice when they were unable to achieve hegemonic strength. In this sense, the hardest blow we received was when Jesuit students of the University of Simeón Cañas decided to leave FAPU, dragging with them FECCAS and a fraction of ANDES. From the first months of 1975 they took part while planning to break off, having achieved sufficient growth in number and organization. Remaining in FAPU no longer much served their interests. They decided to leave us during the cathedral occupation in protest of the massacre of university students, a demonstration which lasted from July 30 to August 6.

The cathedral takeover was an important step for us. National University students demanded that the government provide a higher budget for their alma mater. To pressure the government, they organized a march that left from the university and passed in front of the American Embassy. Near the Social Security building they were intercepted by armored vehicles of the National Guard. General Romero was then the minister of defense. Approximately forty young men and women were massacred. This occurred while I was attending a meeting with a group of Latin American Pastoral Institute alumni where we were discussing the topic of prophecy in conflict situations. The news overwhelmed us and as a response we decided to occupy the cathedral, the first time in the country's history.

During the takeover, several involved held meetings in the cathedral's basement to discuss the creation of the Popular Revolutionary Bloc. These included Choco Ascoli and Alberto Cardenal, Jesuit students; Benito Tovar, Tilo Sánchez, David Rodríguez, and other priests; and the secretaries of FECCAS and other organizations. Mélida Anaya Montes directed their negotiations. They held their first action in front of the cathedral, seizing the moment of civic upheaval. In accordance with their analysis, they were creating a bloc, not a front, because they claimed the country was not mature enough for such a step.

With the departure of those who were now part of the bloc, the remaining members of FAPU were reduced to just a few organizations. We continued our meetings and activities until October and then decided to hold a meeting in Suchitoto to decide whether we would continue or end our project. Mario López, Carlos Arias of National Resistance, and I participated in the meeting. Mario had his own agenda and asked that we continue until December; Carlos wanted to end it immediately. Mario did not share with me his plans to create the Revolutionary Workers Party, and I had no interest in keeping alive something that had already reached its last days. I declared myself in favor of Carlos's position, and then I understood why he proposed what he did. He told us clearly: "We have invested much effort in the Front, we have dedicated many of our people to it. Since as of now the FAPU no longer exists, we want to take it for ourselves, it is our inheritance." Thus, the FAPU did not die but instead became the National Resistance banner.

FAPU thereafter became an instrument of one of the country's leading movements, with the clear purpose of taking political power. The new direction of the second FAPU differed substantially from the social demands and goals we had given to the first. In creating FAPU we had envisioned the formation of a broad popular front able to demand of the government employment, education, health care, better roads, and so forth. Certainly the first FAPU served to raise many people's awareness of the country's problems and to bring together various groups who had not previously known one another.

*Chapter 13*

# Suchitoto: Cradle of Emerging Values

### Cultural Changes among Suchitoto's Campesinos

ACCORDING TO CULTURAL ANTHROPOLOGY, religion makes up a significant portion of many people's values. This seems particularly apt for campesinos. In fact, for campesino communities in which their pastors have had a strong influence, religion forms the leitmotif of community members' lives. The majority of their symbols, values, attitudes, practices, and lifestyles derive from the religious world. After seven years of intense evangelization and awareness-raising based on the Bible, Vatican II, and Medellín, through analysis of our national reality, and the commitment of transformed Salvadorans, of necessity the religion-based value systems sustaining our communities changed. This certainly happened in Suchitoto.

In Suchitoto we witnessed profound changes in the religious arena. Personal piety gave way to a mature, committed faith enlightened by the word of ongoing revelation in history. Moralism focused on sins of sex and alcohol abuse and preaching about death, hell, and heaven gave way to a sacramental morality in which the resurrection took precedence over Christ's Passion and death. Charity was reinterpreted as an obligation to join others in organizing to solve the country's problems, beginning with those in one's own socioeconomic class. The priest, sometimes regarded as a supreme wizard, was demystified. Contributing to this demystification was the celebration of the sacraments in the local language and facing the people during the mass.

We were witnessing the valuing of each person, of individual dignity regardless of possessions or learning. The local people valued the theology of creation and its fulfillment was sought in the theology of baptism. Our daily tasks took on relevance, because we were working, we were creating, we were trying to achieve a true lordship that did not accept oppression or slavery. While affirming individual dignity, we sought to amplify that self-worth within its social, community context. Because of this, we emphasized the need to organize into Christian Base Communities, in trade unions, in the political arena. Both individuality and interpersonal relations were realized. The principle of our ministry was the following: I am a person with everyone else in this place and in this time of history.

The community valued work as an instrument of one's own growth and that of others. Ownership of the means of production does not give us the right to exploit. In a special way, land was valued as the means of the livelihood of all, not of a few who claimed the right to hoard it through the famous, sacred dictum of private property. Land is a social value, as is its transformation. Land's only owner is its Creator; all of the rest of us are users. There was awareness of the need to participate in political struggles, of achieving power. We were not so interested in the vote so much as in true political power as an instrument of cultural and economic power.

Through these ideas, the people developed a nationalist consciousness, meaning being and forming a nation as opposed to continuing in dependency. In particular, they rejected gringo imperialist domination, the usurping of our assets, the offensive and colonialist reference to our nations as "their backyard." That expression means the gringos are in front and we are behind. Therefore, we can be used as a garbage dump for all their crap, which happened quite often with our governments' shameful consent.

It would be beneficial to do an in-depth analysis of the cultural changes that have occurred in the last thirty years and upon these changes build a new foundation for the development of our country as a nation. That could be a job for universities. Throughout these pages I have been pointing out how the spirit of the Suchitoto people has been historically rebellious, yearning for liberty, willing to fight for its dignity. I believe that is what they most value. Suchitoto can be distracted with the electing of queens, with parties and concerts, which is not bad; it helps create a common culture and serves to amuse people, but it is not the people's true soul. Suchitoto's soul is its yearning for freedom as a bastion for the defense of the whole nation. There is its wealth. The symbol of this soul is the indomitable Guazapa Hill.

## SUCHITOTO: CRADLE OF EMERGING VALUES

**Campesino leaders of the Suchitoto parish**
Photo: Cornell Capa (1972)
International Center of Photography, NY City

**Public market in Suchitoto**
Photo: Cornell Capa (1972)
International Center of Photography, NY City

## Cooperatives

During 1976 and part of 1977 we dedicated ourselves, among other things, to contribute to the foundation of collectivized cooperatives. The first one we founded was in San Rafael La Bermuda, some twelve kilometers from Suchitoto. Various members of the Monge families and others whose last names I cannot recall approached me about forming an agricultural cooperative. They had to leave their homes due to the filling of the Cerrón Grande Dam, planned for December 7, 1976.

We had several meetings with them to define the direction they wanted to take with their cooperative, how they would choose to own the land and to work it, and how to distribute the benefits. They all had a good record of organization in FECCAS. After several sessions we decided that a collectivized cooperative would be the most appropriate.

To carry out our project we had to solve a major problem: the purchase of land for thirty-six families. Where would we get the money, if the families had merely the few *colones* CEL would pay them for their possessions? Then I thought about offering them the seventy-five thousand *colones* CEL would pay me for the agricultural school. Unfortunately, that amount was insufficient to acquire at least five *manzanas* per family as well as to build their homes and a community center.

With this problem in mind, I went to visit some friends to ask their advice on how I might obtain other funds. I thought first of Father Antonio Ibáñez, SJ, co-founder of the Salvadoran Foundation for Development and Minimal Housing (FUNDASAL). I supposed he had many contacts abroad to turn to. In a friendly way, the priest suggested I speak with Father Serrano, pastor of the Episcopal Church, who was well connected with Bread for the World in Germany. So I did. Then, without further referrals, I went to the Izalco Travel Agency so that Roger Vega would sell me a ticket on credit to fly to Stuttgart, Germany. I felt sure that if I, a little fellow from the Third World, showed up at the offices of Bread for the World, they would right away help me.

Two days later I found myself on a plane to Germany. As they say, saddle up a horse to go buy bread at the corner store. I found lodging close to the offices of that Lutheran development agency, and early the next morning I was at its door. Ruth Artchur, in charge of Latin America, received me, smiling and curious. Without further ado, she set me down in front of a typewriter so I could put my request in black and white. I almost peed my pants. This was too daring of me. As I had a good understanding of what

I wanted to request, I promptly filled a few sheets asking for one hundred fifty thousand *colones*. We had to build thirty-five houses and a community center, and, according to my calculations, that was the approximate cost. I was even more shocked when three months later I received a check for the amount of sixty thousand US dollars. I think the poor have to be a little daring; after all, it is them Jesus prefers, according to the Gospel.

Money in hand, we bought 172 *manzanas* of land in La Bermuda. I looked for an architecture student at the National University and between the campesinos, he, and I, we designed the houses they wanted. According to our plans, larger families should receive the largest houses and smaller families should occupy the smaller ones.

Later I learned that Bread for the World asked Andrés Gregory to write a report about La Bermuda. In his work he failed to report the seventy-five thousand *colones* I had donated. Later, he once visited me in Managua, because he wanted to be a member-director of the Central American Foundation, of which I was the secretary general and founder. There I complained about his lack of professional ethics. In response he said at the time it was not in his interest to report my donation. Putting politicking above the truth, no matter the damage it does to people!

At first there was a lot of enthusiasm among the cooperative members. Each tried to participate in the decisions made, as well as in carrying them out. People divided themselves according to interests and abilities in various committees to take the work forward. One of these commissions dealt with the marketing of products. Two individuals were entrusted with this work, since they had some experience with it and they knew San Salvador well. However, rather than simply doing this task, they decided to become intermediaries of their own cooperative, while also being buyers. This caused immediate complaints and problems. Realizing cooperative members were upset by their disloyal conduct, they began to forward the idea that it was better to divide the land, to apportion it, that is, to return to the model of individual property. Some, especially young people, welcomed this idea, and the cooperative was divided into two camps.

Individualistic culture runs in our veins; we have been educated in it from generation to generation. Private property is one of the legacies the Spanish left us. In ideological discussions, we can dream as much as we want on this issue, but the reality is that without profound cultural change in our value system, group action remains in the realm of ideas and dreams. With the experience obtained in La Bermuda, other campesinos from Guazapa

Hill approached my brother and me to found two new cooperatives. Of course, we gave them our support and they began to function.

## The Pedagogy of Freire in Cooperatives

It was in these cooperatives that my brother introduced Paulo Freire's pedagogy to educate the members. Several times I accompanied him in his educational sessions, where what was most important was the participation of the campesino men and women. Under my brother's educational guidance, they taught themselves.

Many of them did not know how to read or write, because the prevailing system had not given them that opportunity even though it is so essential to the development of human life. My brother taught them to look at what was around us. In the relationship of the vertical and horizontal lines of a door, for example, we can work out the form of some letters; from an orange's round shape we get countless other letters. In other words, from lines and circles and their combination, we derive the mechanics of making letters. These simple processes of seeing and relating shapes allowed the campesinos to learn, in that first session, what my brother later called "*el OABEDARIO.*" Alongside these campesinos, my brother discovered they could develop an alphabet inspired by their own environment, one differing from the traditional in the letters' order.

Of course, reading and writing does not mean being literate. Something more is needed, to discover why and for what one reads and writes, its political, social, and economic content, and from there to embark on a liberating education. This objective lead to the proposal of an "anthropologic self-educating community." My brother Higinio writes about this:

> The process of anthropologic self-education leads the community to the discovery of its own identity, its values, its capabilities. It is a process that leads from the irrational to the rational; from naiveté to questioning; from the generic to the specific; from the inorganic to the organic; from theory to practice; from 'why do I care?' to commitment; from the unjust to the just; from oppression to liberation.[1]

---

1. H. Alas, Domesticación Escolar y Alternativa, 79.

## The Pedagogy of Freire in Pastoral Work

Along with anthropologic self-education, my brother introduced the pastoral methodology he learned in Riobamba, Ecuador, during his experience at the side of Monsignor Proaño, one of the greatest bishops of Latin America. Monsignor Proaño had in his diocese the dialogic missions, which consisted of applying the method of "pedagogy of the oppressed" to pastoral work with the oppressed. The method consisted mainly in letting the poor speak. The community chose the subject that most interested it, after which someone gave a doctrinal foundation to the chosen topic. They then broke into discussion groups, and later the groups shared what they had discussed with the whole community. This method was always framed in the "see-judge-act" trilogy. But now it was not the "see-judge-act" of others upon a community treated as an object, rather the community acting as a subject in its own right.

It was this very same self-educated community that decided the principal issues around which it would develop its pastoral practice. They thus destroyed power centered in the hands of one or two people, having it absorbed by the entire community, deciding each member's role according to their values. In this way, the authoritarian dictator of the conscience was dispelled and the community gained autonomy.

*Chapter 14*

# Repression Intensifies throughout the Whole Country

## The Region's Political Development

BEGINNING WITH THE OCCUPATION of the cathedral in 1975 and the subsequent creation of the Popular Revolutionary Block, directed by the Popular Forces of Liberation (FPL), the region of Suchitoto overflowed politically. Activists from the five socialist branches were present in the city and in most cantons. Each branch's objective was to bring together the largest number of followers and achieve hegemonic power in the region. Everyone was especially interested in Guazapa Hill, which rises majestically a few kilometers from San Salvador; its north slope leads to Chalatenango, where intensive work was being carried out with the campesinos in the north of that department. Guazapa certainly occupied a strategic location in the country.

During this time my brother and I had remained working in Suchitoto. Due to pressure from the government and some parishioners, Monsignor Chávez had decided to divide our parish into two, as it had been before. The southern cantons belonged to El Calvario and the northern ones to Santa Lucía. Father Armando Recinos, a pious, hard-working, and simple man, had been placed as parish priest of El Calvario. Our pastoral message continued to be centered on the evangelization of our communities, of course, conceiving the Gospel as a message that includes the whole human person. In the political arena, we preferred that the campesinos themselves decide their options. We could not push them to belong to one organization or another, because we did not consider that our role.

In this sense we maintained an independent stance. Our role in the area of faith was to ensure that our people achieved an adult relationship with God and the community. In the human arena, we tried to achieve a "humanization" of the person. We were thus easily accused by the left of supporting a non-dogmatic approach, rather than a prolonged popular war. These charges were made particularly by some members of the FPL, such as Jesuit students, who by then were in the process of leaving the order. Proof of this comes from Carlos Rafael Cabarrús, SJ, who writes in his book *Génesis de una revolución*:

> The Alases, these are two priest brothers and parish priests of Suchitoto, of which Mirandilla is within its jurisdiction; this is a parish distinct from Aguilares parish. These 'progressive' priests allowed various organizations to enter their parish; furthermore, they promoted and supported them. In doing so, they did not show requisite clarity, as they sponsored organizations opposing one another.
>
> It should be remembered that within Aguilares parish the entry of political parties and other organizations was carefully restricted. FECCAS was born and reborn in the very heart of this area, the reason why there was a perfect connection between the religious work done and the fruit that would emerge from it.[1]

Cabarrús is right. The two parishes had different positions, although in all honesty we must remember that the parish priest of Aguilares, Father Rutilio Grande, SJ, did not share his colleagues' stances. We could not, in our role as priests, dedicate ourselves to a single organization, in this case FECCAS, although we supported it the same as the others. It was not our job to define the perfect stance; that was the task of those engaged in politics. I am not here trying to defend myself or my brother or Bernardo Boulang. The reality is that this chapter of Cabarrús, as far as it concerns us, is plagued by a lack of information, and therefore its analysis is incorrect. In his eagerness to extol the work of Aguilares, he goes so far as to argue that FAPU was dependent on the United States and the government.[2]

1. Cabarrús, *Génesis de una revolución*, 203–205.
2. Ibid, 204.

As would be expected given the political context of El Salvador at that time, all of this activity of the parish, of organizations, of alliances with organizations at the national level, forced the government to increase repression. The National Guard, the Hacienda Police, the National Police, and ORDEN dedicated themselves day and night to ruthlessly persecuting the leaders of our communities and the organizations. It was very common in those days for crying women to come to our house very early in the morning to tell us that their husband, son, or daughter had been arrested at midnight or at two in the morning. Sometimes the men of El Zapote, Mirandilla, and Haciendita, had to sleep in the bush, in or near a ravine or gully, to avoid capture by the National Guard. Members of ORDEN had previously identified them as subversives, communists, or enemies of the government. Sometimes the forces of repression simply threw so-called subversives in jail after torturing them at the Guard post; other times they disappeared, or rather, executed, them.

I wonder if women are braver than men. I do not know how to answer this question. The truth is that when one or several men were captured, women came down the mountain to protect their loved ones; they did not abandon them. They dogged the Guards' footsteps as long as necessary to learn their fate. They supported each other and thus cultivated the solidarity of love. Of course, this happened in the early years; later the Guard and other security forces brutalized the populace totally, respecting no one. Children and adults were killed with weapons made by the working men and women of the North, in the name of holy capitalist freedom. Reagan called them "freedom fighters" and my people "beasts." Reagan, in his niche of power, the White House, white on the outside, black on the inside; my people, in their humility, who have only God as a shield of salvation.

Along with our people, we priests also received our share of pain and persecution. Once—I no longer remember the date—they set fire to the back part of our house. It was an old house, large and beautiful, built in the nineteenth century of adobe, wood, and tile. It apparently belonged to one of the Aguilar brothers, a hero of our independence. The fire happened at sundown, when things hide their shapes, enveloped by darkness. For me, the scene was terrible and the smoke asphyxiating. I tried in vain to put out the flames that consumed the roof, with the help of those who were present; the wood was hungry for the fire. Our yard hoses were unable to handle the flames. I wanted to avoid the fire's spreading to Ricardo Leiva's newly built house, but it was impossible. Ricardo lost everything, especially the source of his income, the pharmacy. The fire stopped, as if by the hand of God, just before reaching the warehouse, where he had stored two barrels of alcohol. If those had exploded, the disaster would have been fatal for us all and for the rest of the houses on that block. Who was the criminal? Nobody ever learned. Suchitoto's authorities had no interest in finding out.

On another occasion, someone detonated a homemade bomb at the main gate of our house. As always, the criminal action took place late at night. That time, only my brother, Francisco Rivas, was sleeping in the house. Higinio and I had left; we were in San Salvador. Francisco told me he went to the window right after the explosion and saw only a man running in the darkness; he did not recognize who it was. Wood chips flew everywhere. That night my brother could not sleep. Later I learned who the criminal was, right on an occasion when I had to help him.

## Freed from the National Guard, Thanks to Sex Workers

Sometimes we find help for our physical well-being not from those who are paid to safeguard the security of life, but from someone we would not expect to do so. Even those whose lives are based on social disorder may have compassion. Because of this, I add this event to honor those who one day protected me.

The fields were parched. All nature was showing signs of strain and death, thirsting for rain. It was the time of year when the campesino prepares the soil for the next crop. The heat was stifling, demonic. April in the tropics!

The tractor driver from the school of agriculture arrived at my house and told me: "I am screwed; the tractor has left me stranded in a pasture in Palacios canton. Here is the damaged part that needs replacing. Don Tranquilino, the owner of the land, is worried because the rains are coming soon and he has to plant his corn. I need the replacement part right now." Yet again, the tractor from the school of agriculture needed to be repaired. It was three in the afternoon and immediately I left for San Salvador accompanied by Juan, the tractor driver, a young man about thirty years old, dark skinned and tall, used to days in sun and rain.

We went to different stores and did not find the part. It was almost five in the afternoon, the time when most businesses close, and we decided to return to Suchitoto. Leaving the capital, we spotted a parts store we had not stopped at. I instructed Juan to get out and see if he could find anything there. I added, "I will park alongside Constancia," and I pointed to where

I was going. As I headed to the designated place, I looked in the rearview mirror and realized a police officer was following me. I did not care; all my papers were in order.

I had not finished parking when I saw four National Guard members approaching me, on foot, slowly and staring at my vehicle. I immediately thought that this was not a very suitable place to park and I tried to start the engine I had already turned off. At once their chief came to my window and ordered, "Get out of the vehicle, do not try to run away; please do not make me kill you." The pickup I was driving was surrounded by the four Guards and I could not escape.

The Guard's voice faltered and the tone of his words was pleading. I well understood what he was trying to tell me. I thought of all the campesinos who are Guards, and once in that corps, they received a brainwashing to change all their human and religious values and make them into murderers of the people.

While all this was going on, they had also handcuffed a drunken man who had approached my pickup's right window to ask me for a couple of pennies. I felt bad for the poor man. He had not even finished asking me for those few cents when he was taken prisoner.

The chief ordered me to get out of the vehicle, which I did, taking my time. I needed a few seconds to think about what I might do in this situation. Once on the sidewalk, escorted by the Guards, I began to shout, "I am Father Chencho Alas, parish priest of Suchitoto. Please call Radio Católica and inform them that the Guard has taken me prisoner. Call Monsignor Chávez." I knew the telephone numbers by heart, so I gave them. Facing me, on the other sidewalk, in front of Constancia, there were hundreds of women dedicated to selling their bodies. I had never parked in that place. I did not know Constancia had a Guard post in its own building and that this was the street on which girls had their cubicles to attend to workers and other customers, principally on payday. La Constancia is the only factory in El Salvador that produces beer. It is a monopoly that employs thousands of workers, men and women. It belongs to the Meza Ayau, Quiñónez and Murray families.

The chief shouted at me: "Shut up or I will kill you." I replied, "This is my only defense, to give the phone numbers of Monsignor and the radio; I will not be quiet." He hit me on the back with his rifle, trying not to hurt me. I was lucky; I had fallen into the hands of a reasonable man, who was following orders but without malice.

## REPRESSION INTENSIFIES THROUGHOUT THE WHOLE COUNTRY

The women began to shout all sorts of insults at the Guards. Their repertoire of profanity was bountiful and classic. Cervantes would have been jealous. Bastards, motherfuckers, assholes, shitheads echoed from wall to wall. The Guards always had the women there in front of them, across the street, and they paid them no attention. Besides, there were so many of them. Never in my life had I seen so many young women together, in their little dresses that did not hide what they were offering.

I moved forward slowly and they forced me to enter the Guard post. They asked me to sit. I thought they were going to interrogate me, as on other occasions, but it was not like that. What they did was to tie my thumbs together with a nylon cord. They did it without any mercy. Right away my thumbs became inflamed due to lack of circulation, and I began to feel a sharp pain running up both my arms, something indescribable. Then they tied my feet to two chains. They were so thick I thought an elephant would be unable to break them. They had gone overboard. I remained sitting there for more than two hours without anybody approaching to tell me anything, although they were watching me.

After that, two individuals in civilian dress abruptly entered. They showed their credentials to the guards watching me and then approached me. Their faces were extremely distorted and their eyes glazed. I thought they looked like rabid dogs. They were from the G2, Chele Medrano's secret guard. They were evidently on drugs. One of them said to me, "All right, motherfucker, son of a bitch, now we have you. You have finally fallen. We have eagerly and joyfully awaited this moment. Now we have got you. We are going to take you to the Lempa River, in Suchitoto, your land, and there we are going to tie a rock around your neck and drown you in the river. Sonofabitch, you never stop screwing around with your sermons on agrarian reform and other bullshit." He then threatened to hit me, but the post chief stopped him. He said to him, "Do not touch him, this case is already resolved. Soon they are coming to take him to headquarters." The G2 looked at me with hatred in his eyes and backed away threateningly.

A half hour later a Guard captain, whom I knew, arrived dressed as a civilian. He had been the chief in Suchitoto. He was a member of INTERPOL in El Salvador. He was short, of muscular build, with the face of a cunning animal. His friends called him *El Pajarito*. At the time he was working at Guard headquarters, which I learned hours later. He spoke with the chief of the post and then approached me, ordering them to free my thumbs and feet. The Guard who carried out his order had difficulty freeing my thumbs.

The nylon had become enmeshed in my swollen flesh and could not be seen. If he cut the nylon, he had to injure me. The operation of untying me completed, El Pajarito said to me, "Do not worry, you are free to go. Monsignor Chávez has already spoken with the president and all is settled. Nevertheless, I must take you to headquarters, so you can sign the release order we are going to give you." I obeyed without responding. With this kind of person, it is better to keep your mouth shut, whenever possible.

We went outside and my astonishment was enormous. Across the street at least two hundred young women dressed in colorful getups had gotten together, their faces painted up in the way that revealed their line of work. Again they rained down on the Guard all types of insults and threats. Some of them showed signs of anger and hatred for the Guards.

Just as El Pajarito started his car, my brother Sabino, a lawyer, arrived. I told him where the INTERPOL captain was taking me. He followed me closely, until I went through the barracks' gates. My brother has never abandoned me in my life's difficult moments; he has always been with me, supporting me. He has been faithful and brave.

El Pajarito made remarks along the way, as if nothing had happened. For him everything was normal. Once at headquarters, they took me to a large office, full of officials, where they offered me a cup of coffee. I did not accept it. They offered me, in a mocking tone, some milk, and as they gave it to me, they commented, "Do not worry, it is not poisoned; we are not going to kill you." I drank the milk calmly. After all, I was really thirsty. If they had not done anything to me before, they would not do it now. Then they made me sign a document stating they had treated me with kindness, without hurting me, morally or physically.

They made me wait a few minutes until Father Nemesio Chinchilla came to pick me up. Chinchilla had been a classmate of General Romero, who by that time was president of the country, and had negotiated my freedom with him. Chinchilla took me to the San José de la Montaña Seminary, where Monsignor Rivera and two or three other priests awaited me, having heard about my capture on Radio Católica.

I was about to say goodbye to Monsignor Rivera when a Dominican priest arrived. Elatedly, he told me how he had heard about what happened. He was working in his office in his church, El Rosario, downtown, when two women who had witnessed my capture came to see him. They said, "Father, they have taken Father Chencho Alas prisoner. He yelled at us to go see the archbishop to give him the news about what was going on. But as you can see, Father, dressed like this, the archbishop is not going to receive us." And they gave a half turn and showed him their red panties, extremely short. If not for these women, I probably would not have escaped torture and perhaps even death.

## My Last Encounter with Rutilio Grande

Rutilio Grande, like me, was of campesino origin. He was born in El Paisnal, in the department of San Salvador, and I in Chiapas, in Chalatenango department. It was the same archbishop, the kindly Monsignor Luis Chávez y González, who brought us both to the seminary. Shortly after he entered the seminary, Rutilio joined the Jesuits, and I, wanting to be a diocesan priest, continued my studies. Rutilio worked in the Jesuit schools and later in the seminary until he was promoted to parish priest of Aguilares. Rutilio wanted to dedicate his last years in complete service to the people, and so he did.

He was much helped in deciding to work directly with the people by Father Jesús Ángel Bengochea, a Spanish Jesuit who came to work with me in 1971. Jesús Ángel and Rutilio had planned to work together in a rural parish. It was this idea that led Rutilio to study pastoral work, as I had previously, at the Latin American Pastoral Institute (IPLA), in Quito, Ecuador. There he was a classmate of my brother Higinio for most of 1972. While Rutilio was in Quito, Jesús Ángel came and asked me to talk with Father Francisco Estrada, his provincial leader, to convince him of the importance of Jesuits working in the countryside.

By then some of the campesino organizations had advanced quite well, and there was good pastoral development in several of the country's rural parishes. Most of these parishes were located in the archdiocese. It was a time of tremendous blossoming of diocesan clergy and their parishes. The one who allowed, supported, and promoted this growth was Monsignor Luis Chávez y González.

The two of us went to visit Francisco Estrada, whom I had known since childhood, because he also began his life as a postulant to the priesthood at the San José de la Montaña Seminary. During the meeting, Jesús Ángel was a little nervous but very happy. I tried to convince Francisco of the importance of a Jesuit presence in the countryside. I had several arguments in favor of my proposal. I remember two of them. The first argument was the significance of a Jesuit working with campesinos. The Jesuits enjoy an almost mythical reputation, earned through generations of men dedicated to fulfilling their duties with dedication and depth. According to the middle and upper classes, the Jesuits belong to them; they are their intellectual servants. The second argument was that, among the Jesuits, there are specialists in different fields, which allows them to form teams, thus providing a model for us diocesan priests who usually work in isolation. Francisco listened to me with interest. He probably already had an idea of what we were going to say. Several months later, in September 1972, we received the good news that Rutilio had been assigned to Aguilares and that this rural parish was being handed over to the Jesuits.

Because Rutilio was my parish neighbor, I visited him from time to time. We especially spoke together at the clergy's monthly meetings. Sometimes he seemed depressed or tired to me, and on one occasion he even confided in me his desire to leave the parish. His pastoral line clashed with the positions of his colleagues, who had a defined political agenda. The situation worsened after the founding of the Popular Revolutionary Bloc. He saw how many of its leaders were falling, victims of repression, and this distressed him.

He knew that the church has a prophetic role, and he did not accept its subordination to factional interests. The prophetic role is above ideologies and therefore enjoys freedom; it is not tied to a particular party or class. The prophet denounces evil wherever it is found and announces the Kingdom to all, particularly to the poor, because they have a more hopeful attitude, having nothing to lean on in the earthly city. Rutilio bore this anguish until the end of his life.

Rutilio was a member of the commission of the liturgy of which Monsignor Rivera Damas was president, and I the secretary. His participation was highly esteemed by all. On Tuesday, March 8, 1977, we had our customary afternoon meeting at the seminary, which at the time also served as the archbishop's headquarters. After the session, as I stood in the wide corridor off the basketball court, Rutillio came up to me and hugged me. He was very emotional, and accompanied his hug with a phrase: "Chencho, I think I am leaving for good."

I asked if he was leaving the country or whether he was leaving the archdiocese. Given the political situation of the time, and the state of persecution of the church, of popular organizations and their leaders, it was quite possible that Rutilio wanted to leave Aguilares to go work elsewhere, even to another country. Rutilio, it should be kept in mind, was a relatively timid man. He responded, "No, Chencho, I am not leaving Aguilares. I think this time something more serious is going to happen, and I am leaving for good." Right away

I understood Rutilio's message. His words and hug personally moved me. In his face, in his words, there was a mix of anxiety, resignation, agitation; he both accepted and rejected the facts at the same time. For me, it was like he was on hold, knowing yet not knowing what was coming, a premonition of his life's denouement. We parted, each with our own fears, each accepting the risks, each full of hopes and uncertainties. That was my farewell to Rutilio, a great friend. The fruit of the tree of his life had matured; it was ready for the harvest in the Lord's vineyard, and he was ready to leave.

Rutilio had received death threats on several occasions, and the situation in Aguilares was very volatile. The volatility was due to the degree of belligerency of the area's campesino organizations, especially FECCAS. Their burning of cane fields and bales of cane bagasse stored in the San Francisco sugar mill had infuriated the general manager, Kurt Nottebohn, a German who had arrived from Guatemala fleeing the timid agrarian reform carried out by Jacobo Arbenz in 1953. The bales were intended to serve as raw material for the manufacture of indoor building partitions. The San Francisco manager had planned to convert the mill into an agribusiness conglomerate, as he himself had told me.

One day during that period I had a meeting with Nottebohn in his San Salvador offices. I went to ask him, in his capacity as a director of the Agricultural Development Bank, for a letter on behalf of a group of campesinos of Cerro de Guazapa who wanted to buy a piece of land to form a cooperative. He came to me full of uncontrollable rage. He shouted at me, "Again these campesinos of the Jesuits have burned my cane fields and all the bales I had stored. Those criminals need a lesson I will give them." His chin trembled, his face so enraged it looked like right then and there he was going to explode of a heart attack or stroke.

On Saturday, March 12, 1977, on the road to El Paisnal, Rutilio's birthplace, a death squad waited for him, rifles in hand. It was the hour of sacrifice, at sundown, on the banks of the cane fields, symbol of our campesinos' enslavement. He died in the arms of the cane, which he had denounced so often as an emblem of exploitation. After mass in the cathedral, we had another funeral service in Aguilares and then, in procession, we carried Father Rutilio's body to El Paisnal for burial in the church. Although I was afraid to participate due to the persecution I was experiencing, I decided to accompany Rutilio in those last moments. In my mind I have always believed the cane growers were behind this murder. It was they who were interested in the death of an innocent.

*Chapter 15*

# Monsignor Romero
*Pastor, Prophet, and Martyr*

### Introductory Note

THIS IS A SPECIAL chapter for me, dealing with my last days in El Salvador. Before relating the events that led to my leaving Suchitoto, I want this chapter to serve as my personal testimony of Archbishop Oscar Romero. I think he is a martyr and a saint, and above all, the greatest symbol of my people's dream for justice and peace. He symbolizes our best ideals and our hopes. I wrote this chapter in Nicaragua during my years of exile in that beautiful country for which I wish the greatest good fortune.

### This Chapter's Scope

It is not easy for me to write about Archbishop Romero. Too many events and words rush to mind, all related to his life and the lives of the Salvadoran people. Without any pretension, I want to tell you about a few of these happenings and words that left a mark on his personhood and gave a new historical meaning to the church and to our country, which he served. I do not claim to make a theological analysis or present a systematization of his eminently prophetic ministry. That is the work of experts in the fields of biblical studies, theology, and ministry.

## Background of the Conversion

On February 22, 1977, Monsignor Romero became the heir of Monsignor Luis Chávez y González, archbishop of San Salvador, who had propelled the archdiocese into a ministry inspired by the Gospel, Vatican II, and the Second Conference of Latin American Bishops. Monsignor Chávez, who served as archbishop from 1939 to 1977, was neither a brilliant intellectual nor a theologian, of European cut or of liberation, but rather a pastor. Whenever there was an event related to church renewal, inside or outside the country, Chávez always attended and immediately saw how he might apply its conclusions to his parishes. He was a practical man, completely dedicated to seeking the welfare of the sheep entrusted to his ministry. Romero, who followed him as archbishop, would not have become our prophet and martyr were it not for the rich pastoral heritage left by Chávez. What most motivated Romero to change was the ample number of diocesan clergy and laity committed to the Gospel and its implications. In my case, without Archbishop Chávez's strong support, I would not have been able to develop and carry out my ministry in Suchitoto.

VUELVEN A SUCHITOTO. Los padres Higinio y José Inocencio Alas (4° y 7°., de izquierda a derecha), regresaron el sábado a hacerse cargo nuevamente de la parroquia, después de varios días de ausencia por la orden de captura que existía contra ambos, en un juicio de incitación al pueblo que se sigue en el Juzgado de aquella ciudad. Los dos sacerdotes llegaron acompañados de Monseñor Oscar A. Romero y de familiares de ambos. (Foto de Alvarez).

Blessed Mons. Oscar Romero, my brothers, and 15,000 people
Freed from political accusations
Photo: CoLatino

Land, Liberation, and Death Squads

## The Beginning of a Conversion

The day of Father Rutilio Grande's assassination, March 12, 1977, was not an easy day for the new archbishop of San Salvador. That day a wave rolled in that would grow throughout the week, cresting on March 19 before crashing on March 20. A whole week of events forced Romero to question his own values and respond to the demands of his people and their partners: priests, members of religious orders, community leaders, and catechists. On March 12, he fell from his horse, like Saint Paul; on March 19 he questioned his theological understanding of "authority and obedience," and on March 20, he gave himself over and was consecrated, during a mass, as the people's prophet. After March 20, his life continued for three more years until he celebrated another mass at 5:30 p.m. on March 24, 1980, the date on which he delivered himself for eternity to the God of Life.

As detailed previously, I had been friends with Monsignor Romero since 1962. After he attended my second cursillo de Cristiandad, we often gave the workshops together. I spent the last three months of my ministry in Suchitoto, March through May 1977, working for the archbishop in the San José de la Montaña Seminary. Our friendship and my work allowed me to get close to him as a person.

On February 28, 1977, the army massacred dozens of government opponents both inside and outside the Church of the Rosary, located in the heart of the city opposite Parque Libertad. The night before, Father Alfonso Navarro had celebrated mass for the ten thousand people assembled in the park to protest the fraudulent presidential election of February 20. The cold-blooded massacre was part of a government policy to crush the demands of the people, who since 1967 had been seeking various ways to organize to fight for a decent life. The economic development model launched by the Alliance for Progress in the Kennedy era had run its course, and people were hungrier than ever. Hundreds of catechists, labor leaders, campesinos, women, and children who demanded rights had been systemically assassinated.

On that fateful February 28, a mere six days after Monsignor Romero had become archbishop of San Salvador, we began a weeklong workshop on the growth of fundamentalist Protestant sects in Latin America. Before the sessions, some of us clergy had met and tasked Rutilio with addressing the bishops to insist that they face what was happening in our country with prophetic leadership. Present at his address were the new archbishop, Monsignor Oscar Romero; the departing archbishop, Monsignor Luis Chávez y

González; and the auxiliary bishop, Monsignor Arturo Rivera Damas. As a result of Rutilio's presentation, the bishops pledged to write a pastoral letter. In addition, we priests decided to return to our parishes to be with our people during this difficult time rather than attend the workshop on Protestantism. It was the bishops' pastoral letter that Rutilio had planned to read the day he was martyred. It denounced the violence against the campesinos, the destruction of their crops, the murders of their leaders—or, the same thing, their disappearances—the intimidating media campaigns by organizations like the Association of Private Enterprise (ANEP) and the Eastern Region Agricultural Front (FARO) against the church, the expulsion of some priests from the country, and other outrages. After Father Grande and his two companions, an old man and a boy, both campesinos. were buried in El Paisnal, Monsignor Romero agreed to call together the clergy, religious orders, and some lay people to analyze the situation more calmly and to take action to exert the church's prophetic mission at that time.

Romero had the spiritual disposition to work with the inheritance he had received from Monsignor Chávez. Namely, he received a committed church, enlarged by its acceptance and implementation of the Second Vatican Council, and, in particular, by putting into practice the teachings of the Second Conference of Latin American Bishops in Medellín. On February 21, the day before he took possession of the Archdiocese of San Salvador, Romero wrote to the clergy, "I wish to speak with you about the spirit of cooperation I offer you and need from you, so that together we can participate in the honor Christ gives us to help build his church, each according to his calling."

On the afternoon of March 17, Romero had to make this spirit of cooperation reality. From March 13 to 16, several priests had met twice with him. He had sought dialogue on the following four points: the basic elements on which we should stand united so that the church could present a common position; actions with which we were all in agreement; an assessment of the public opinion the church had been able to create through the bishops' radio messages, newsletters, and other means; and other suggestions and items of discussion.

## The Celebration of a Single Mass

In the plenary meeting on that March 17, we participants could vote on the different proposals presented. However, due to his theological training, the archbishop maintained that our votes carried only the weight of advice. Among the proposals, one in particular caused quite a stir: to celebrate just one mass in the archdiocese on Sunday, March 20, to be presided over by the archbishop and accompanied by all the priests and people of the archdiocese. There would be no masses in individual parishes.

There were two fundamental issues that troubled the archbishop about such a mass, one legal and the other theological. Legally, the country was under a state of siege and one could not hold outdoor public activities without government permission. Theologically, we had been taught that each mass contributed to building God's glory: a mathematical conception of the sacrament of unity and love.

In San Salvador, we were accustomed to innovation with Monsignor Chávez. His pastoral motto had been, "If something will serve the good of the people, let us go ahead and do it." However, for Monsignor Romero, in the country's circumstances it seemed unacceptable to hold only one mass as well as contrary to his doctrinal way of thinking.

After seeking private advice and being hounded by diocesan clergy trained under Monsignor Chávez, all of whom were committed to working with and on behalf of the poor, the archbishop agreed to hold the single mass. Nonetheless, among many dissenters stood one particularly important opponent: the Nuncio Gerarda, the representative of His Holiness the Roman Pontiff in El Salvador. Ivan Illich said it well: it is difficult for a diplomat to be a Christian, whether the diplomat represents the Vatican or the United States. Indeed, it is difficult for him to be a prophet, an essential element of baptism.[1]

On Saturday, at two in the afternoon, the nuncio arrived at San José de la Montaña Seminary, where the archbishop had his provisional offices. Some seminarians, my sisters, and I were preparing signs for each parish to use during the mass. We had planned that the faithful would organize according to their parishes in the plaza in front of the cathedral. The nuncio seemed very worried to me. He asked for the archbishop, and I told him that he was not in. He looked angry and said, "He should be here. Tomorrow is a terrible day for the church and it is his duty to be here. Available." He gave me a letter for the archbishop and left.

---

1. Theologically, when a person receives baptism she or he is called upon to be a prophet: to decry injustices in society and help to bring about the reign of God here on Earth.

Romero was out praying with some members of Opus Dei. He was a man of prayer, and the conservative positions of Opus Dei, a sect within the Catholic Church, attracted him. Opus cultivates piety, does not question the status quo, and works for the salvation of society's leaders, for the lords of capital. With a Hellenic mentality, they succeed in separating historical reality from ideas and are dedicated to proclaiming the latter. Thus, they evade any sort of commitment.

Monsignor returned to the seminary at five thirty, and I immediately gave him the nuncio's letter. He went to his room for five minutes, then returned and asked me to read it. In his role as a representative of the Holy See, the nuncio warned Romero to halt the mass scheduled for the following day. He asked him to make a radio announcement that all clergy remain in their parishes.

## The Hour of the Conversion

For me, this was Romero's zero hour, the hour of his conversion. Perhaps it had begun in Tres Calles, when he saw the blood of the campesinos assassinated by the National Guard. For some years, our people's blood had been spilling around him, crying out for his conversion. On June 21, 1975, the National Guard had surrounded the village of Tres Calles. It is located in the Santiago de María diocese, where Romero was bishop at the time. The Guardsmen accused five campesinos of storing arms for the guerillas; they pulled them from their huts and massacred them. The next day, Monsignor visited the hamlet to console the families and celebrate mass.

For the first time, the campesinos' blood was in front of him, beseeching him, questioning him. His response was that of a good man, a good bishop. He wrote a letter to President Molina and a memorandum to his colleagues, the bishops. In a way, he felt committed to doing this because he had gone to Tres Calles, along with several priests of the San Vicente Diocese. In the memo he explained why he did not make a public protest: it seemed better to intervene directly with the authorities, as he had done, personally protesting to the military commander and writing to the president. He added that the church was not directly involved in the matter and that he was unsure of the true motives for the massacre and the victims' behavior. This procedure is called diplomatic silence. This deed and other happenings in the country, however, were seriously calling out to Romero's conscience. The spilled blood was that of the poor, just like his blood.

## Land, Liberation, and Death Squads

No one knows if Tres Calles reminded him of his campesino upbringing. Oscar Arnulfo Romero Galdámez was born in Ciudad Barrios, in San Miguel department, on August 15, 1917. He was the son of a telegraph operator and postal worker named Santos Romero and of Guadalupe de Jesús Galdámez, a teacher and seamstress. Oscar learned the trade of carpentry before entering the seminary. Back then, Ciudad Barrios, only twenty kilometers from the Honduran border, was just a large hamlet, with dusty streets in the dry season and muddy streets in the rainy. Romero knew country life firsthand.

On that March 19, 1977, the nuncio's letter telling Romero to stop the following day's single mass also spoke to his conscience. The nuncio's missive was full of clerical authoritarianism, and for a moment, I feared all was lost. At stake was the concept of obedience to authority Romero had learned in the Gregorian University's classrooms during World War II, in the epoch of the noble Pius XII.

Personally, I believe Romero had everything necessary to commit himself to the people, like many of us who worked at that time in about forty parishes. Simple people, inspired, self-sacrificing, followers of the Gospel, of Vatican II and Medellín, priests who knew their people. The majority of these priests belonged to the Archdiocese of San Salvador. But the problem Monsignor Romero faced was theological in nature; it had to do with his ideas about authority and his sense of obedience. On the one hand, the church's doctrine is clear; on the other, there are those who believe they are the final authority of the doctrine in daily practice. How could he say no to the nuncio? That was impossible.

I read the nuncio's letter, and Romero, worried and nervous, asked me what he should do. It was early evening and we were leaning on the handrail in the hall of the seminary, a simple and beautiful building. Romero was suffering. I reminded him of theology. I spoke to him of his mission as a pastor and as bishop. This did not move him.

I reminded him of something he himself had said when we gave cursillos de Cristiandad together years earlier: "If we have a problem and do not know what to do, what decision to make, the best thing to do is go talk with Jesus." I suggested that he go to the seminary chapel to speak with Jesus. I watched him walk slowly and calmly to the chapel. He crossed the building from south to north, through the wide central hall festooned with bougainvillea, full of flowers and thorns, a symbol of life, and he entered the chapel. The silence of the sacred invites us to make the best decisions of our life.

About an hour later, Romero returned down the same hall, approaching me. His face was serene and peaceful, and he had a smile on his lips. He said, "Tomorrow we will all be in the cathedral where we will celebrate mass together." This was his break with the past. The decision forced him to define his own identity and to accept his destiny as pastor, as the person responsible for the inheritance he had received as archbishop.

Late in the night of March 19, Romero wanted to review the introduction I had prepared for the mass. He invited me to the house of Father Jesús Delgado, whom he esteemed for his theological knowledge. Jesús was a professor at the UCA, the Jesuit university. We had foreseen that before the mass began the following day, parishioners would be arriving a few at a time from all the archdiocesan parishes and from other dioceses. We planned to use loudspeakers to prepare the faithful as they filled Barrios plaza in front of the cathedral.

In preparing his message, it was easy to prophetically denounce the assassination of Rutilio and his two companions, and to point out the intellectual authors of the murders. All that was needed was to weave together quotations from the Bible, from Vatican II and Medellín documents, from bishops' letters and declarations made by the extreme right in the newspapers. Romero began to read us the text slowly. He seemed to be a tailor, snipping here and there. The forty-minute introduction was shortened to twenty. He feared hurting someone, causing problems, and above all, he wanted to be sure that everything in the mass was under his control.

We slept very little that night. Romero went to bed exhausted. It was three in the morning and the mass would begin at nine. At the appointed hour on March 20, we all went to the cathedral. It was Sunday, the Lord's Day. We found a sea of people before us; the plaza had filled up little by little. People came from everywhere, without caring about the state of emergency the government had decreed a few days earlier.

We began with the introduction to the mass, but Monsignor Romero quickly interrupted. He put on the celebratory vestments and, without giving the seminarians or me time to finish, he began with the invocation: "In the name of the Father, of the Son, and of the Holy Spirit." Many things have been done in the church and my country beginning with the invocation of the Trinity, but very few have had such a repercussion or so powerfully affirmed love between us. In fact, the invocation has been used many times to bless tools of death, guns, which have murdered eighty thousand people in my country. In the name of God, one can even be anti-communist.

When Monsignor Romero began the mass he was sweaty, pale, and nervous. Once the readings ended, he leaned on his staff and began his sermon. He was an elegant preacher, known among the clergy for his ability. He had a good command of the language. I remember that his sermon began slowly, heavily. He sought the rhythm of the words. He looked tired and without the desire to face the challenge of the crowd standing in front of him. It is not easy to make the leap from a generous man to a prophet. The prophet is like the people's soul: he or she knows their pain and anguish and carries to everyone the hope of Jesus's death and resurrection. The people were asking that of him.

Little by little, he let himself be carried by the people's spirit. He began to denounce sin, the structures of sin and crime, and then, moved by God's Spirit, to announce the Kingdom. It was the moment of his confirmation. Overcome by that Spirit, he became a prophet forever. He accepted something more than martyrdom. From then on, he began living the pain and hope of El Salvador. He made his own the widow's weeping, the orphan's begging bread, the young people's search for freedom, and the nation's struggle; he gave them all the transcendence that comes from the Kingdom. I would say that Monsignor Romero was converted during that sermon, in front of what is the most sacred component of a nation: its people.

## Pastor, Prophet, and People

From that great community mass on, Romero became the pastor-prophet. Children, teenagers, women, widows, workers, students, teachers, professionals, oligarchs, members of religious orders, and priests sought him out. He was the man who offered silence to listen and words to console, to illuminate a solution to a conflict, to encourage.

Simultaneously, a campaign against him began. Those who had pressured the authorities for Romero's nomination as archbishop felt betrayed, including more than one bishop. They tried to bypass him, they manipulated their offices so as to isolate him from the people, and they used his position as archbishop to make him leave his simple room at the seminary.

For example, early one morning in April 1977, a woman of the upper middle-class wanted to speak with the archbishop. But right at that moment he was busy, headed for his office to meet with some campesinos who had come to tell him about their situation in northern Chalatenango. His preference was for the poor. Romero approached me and said, "Speak with this woman. I need to see to this group of campesinos who wait for me; they have come from far away and need me." I spoke with the woman who, by the way, was the mother of an old friend of mine. She lamented not being able to speak with Monsignor, because she had an important message for him. She told me that a group of friends had met and decided to find him a dwelling worthy of his position: a mansion. Don Rafael Meza Ayau, owner of the beer monopoly, had sent her to offer him a furnished residence in the Escalón neighborhood worthy of his dignity. At lunch I gave him the message and he replied, "They want to separate me from the people." He paused and added, "After all, what is a bishop's dignity? Of what does it consist?"

I would say that Romero's first reaction after the March 20 mass was to immerse himself in the people, to feel their presence in a new and deeper way, bathe himself in their lives, drink of their words and deeds. It is as if he went through a new baptism.

Throughout the week he listened to the concerns people brought him. On Sundays and even some weekdays he communicated his experiences with everyone in the mass, particularly during the homily, which was transmitted by radio so the whole nation could hear it. People in the city and countryside listened to him. His words even echoed in the oligarchs' homes who listened to him either with rage or happiness, depending on their ideological position. I think the transistor radio caused the first cultural revolution in Third World countries. That certainly happened in El Salvador. I have seen families who lived in huts with little more than a roof who had a transistor radio hanging from a post, playing at full blast for hours. I have seen campesinos riding their emaciated horses with a transistor radio hanging from the saddle. They have no money for food, but they do for batteries. Their world thirsts for music, words, and news.

Monsignor Romero, who frequently visited their villages, knew about this thirst and how to put it to good use. Each weekday evening he spent fifteen minutes of his time sharing a short radio message. For many, he was their only contact with the outside world, letting them know what was going on in the country.

I remember him on the first nights of his ministry as archbishop, discussing his message with Father Gregorio Rosa Chávez (later auxiliary bishop of San Salvador) or me. There was so much to say! He knew that, in order to respect the people, his message would have to be educational, to slowly build the people's awareness.

Their consciousness did grow during his three years as archbishop, an awareness that became more critical each day in the face of the reality of their lives and the country's power structures. This consciousness brought people to organize themselves in a thousand ways, often through Christian Base Communities. With Romero, the Christian Base Communities grew horizontally and vertically.

A deep and close relationship developed between Archbishop Romero and his people, as can be seen in the letters he received. They were letters of a people to their pastor. In the church, we are used to and even interested in reading the pope's letters to the faithful, the bishops' to their flocks. We do not realize there is a whole theology fed by the Spirit, of a very pastoral nature, in the letters of the people to their bishop. Monsignor Romero read them. It was the communion of the pastor with his sheep, the communion of the saints. They were letters written by hands used to the machete or to washing *nixtamal*[2] by the side of the river. They came from women and men of the countryside, workers in the slums, from the affluent in uptown neighborhoods. The letters spoke of their struggles, their hopes, their confidence in him. They encouraged him and sustained his faith. A bishop also needs support to maintain faith and hope. A bishop without hope is not a bishop; he is just a church employee with a hierarchical title, nothing more.

The letters make plain this close connection between Romero and the people. For example, one parishioner wrote to him, "I always listen to YSAX radio and my faith grows daily because I never before felt that the church was so close to us poor people." A group added, "Bishop, we want to let you know that your preaching and homilies move us to keep going stronger and more enthusiastically in this struggle to build a more just order, beginning with ourselves." Some letters noted the unity of the pastor and his church: "We, the Christian community, committed to Jesus Christ, are one with you and are very happy to have a pastor and prophet in our times."

From these people Romero learned language that gave life to his words. At times, seeking a better way to explain the corrupt administration of justice in the country, he could find a no more precise phrase than one he had learned from a campesino: "The law is like a snake, it only bites the barefoot."

---

2. Corn boiled with lime, and then washed before grinding into tortilla dough.

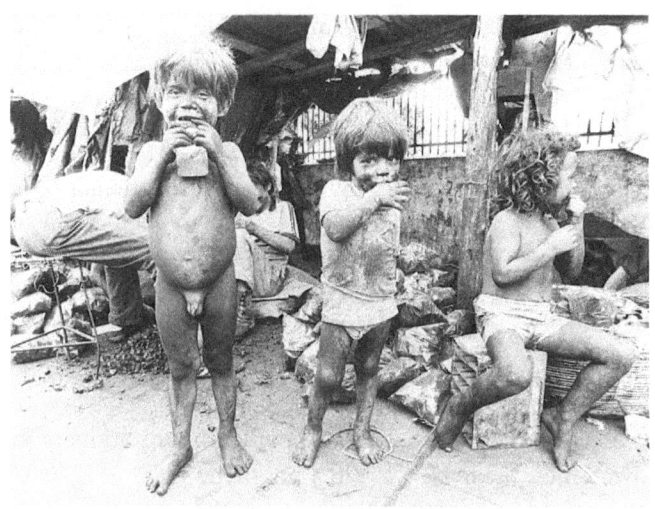

They need us; we need them
Photo: Cornell Capa (1972)
International Center of Photography, NY City

## Messenger of Life for Youth

For many post–Vatican II bishops and pastors, the lack of new people entering the priesthood and religious life in general has been a big headache. Many seminaries have had to close. Young people have refused to lead a life that only offers privation, within an unproductive bureaucracy that gives little sense of challenge. The priest's identity, as a human being and as a pastor, has not always been clear. Monsignor Romero gave it a new dimension for many youth. Many felt attracted to his prophetic vision of life. They approached him to dialogue and found in him a source of inspiration, someone whose mission they could follow. The seminary, which had been empty when he became archbishop, filled to the point they had to turn many youth away for lack of space. Romero was a messenger of life, and this filled the people.

## The Popular Organizations and Violence

From the beginning of his ministry in San Salvador, Romero worried about the conflict between people's right to organize and violence. He dedicated his third pastoral letter to this subject. It was the fruit of a dialogue with priests, political leaders, workers, campesinos, teachers, and other groups in Salvadoran society. Monsignor Arturo Rivera Damas, bishop of Santiago de María (and later archbishop of San Salvador), wrote the letter jointly with him. They wrote:

> The situation in our country and the continual questioning by our Christians, especially the campesinos, compels us to illuminate with urgency and as much as we possibly can these two problems: the so-called "popular organizations," which could benefit from more accurate descriptions, according to their nature and objectives; and the problem of violence, which every day needs further distinctions and classifications of prudent Christian morality.[3]

The two bishops confirmed that "popular organizations" were proliferating. No doubt, the presence of the prophetic word in El Salvador had created the need for people to organize to make way for just solutions to society's problems.

The right to carry out such organizing had been denied. Monsignor alluded to the institutionalized violence resulting from the reality that economically powerful minorities could organize to defend their minority interests, but workers, campesinos, and teachers faced only difficulties and even repression. Even worse, the powerful encouraged confrontation among the groups, especially among the campesinos. They added that, in El Salvador, "that which has forced them to organize in the first place is not merely the civic right to participate in the country's economic and political affairs, but rather the simple vital necessity to survive, to exercise their rights so that their lives become at least tolerable."[4] What people seek is to avoid remaining at life's margin. Romero and Rivera defended life itself, especially the lives of the most vulnerable. For that same reason they denounced violence. This denunciation of violence and affirmation of life is what definitively carried Monsignor Romero to his martyrdom. One need only remember his famous homily given in the cathedral on March 23, 1980, one day before his death:

> I would like to appeal in a special way to the army's enlisted men, and in particular to the ranks of the Nacional Guard and the police—those in the barracks. Brothers! You are of part of our own people! You kill your own campesino brothers and sisters. Before

---

3. Romero and Rivera Damas, "The Church and Popular Political Organizations," 3.
4. Ibid, 6.

an order to kill that a man may give, God's law must prevail: *Thou shalt not kill!*

No soldier is obliged to obey an order against the law of God. No one has to fulfill an immoral law. It is time to take back your consciences and to obey your consciences rather than the orders of sin. The church, defender of the rights of God, of the law of God, of human dignity, of the person, cannot remain silent before such abominations. We want the government to understand seriously that reforms are worth nothing if they are stained with so much blood.

In the name of God, and in the name of this suffering people, whose laments rise to heaven each day more tumultuous, I beg you, I beseech you, I order you in the name of God: Stop the repression![5]

Monsignor Romero understood the value of human life, which he himself lost. In early January 1980, I had a short conversation with him in the Divine Providence Hospital. He told me about the threats he received every day, of the possibility of he himself also falling into the furrow, of giving his life for the people. As he spoke, his face showed anguish and sadness. There was nothing easy about facing the consequences of being a prophet. Jesus himself was afraid on the Mount of Olives.

Romero gave up his life on March 24. The last words he spoke during the mass that day, a memorial service for Doña Sara de Pinto, owner of the *Independent Daily* newspaper, were the following:

> May this body immolated and this blood sacrificed for humans nourish us also, so that we may give our body and our blood to suffering and to pain—like Christ, not for self, but to bring about justice and peace for our people. Let us join together, then, intimately in faith and hope at this moment of prayer for Doña Sarita and ourselves.

Romero was segueing from the sermon into the offertory when a bullet struck his heart. His body and his blood, the bread and wine, converted themselves in that instant into one single offering to God. It was an offering of passion, of death, one which will realize full life when the people of El Salvador and Central America are freed from injustice and live in peace. At that time Monsignor Romero will be resurrected. His resurrection is

---

5. The final address of Romero has been published widely and may be easily found online. Even the English-language feature film *Romero* from 1989 contains these lines from Romero's final homily.

anticipated in time and in space, it is an eschatological resurrection because it bears the stamp of the alliance the archbishop made with the people and with our God.

This offering will join many other offerings of lives, the blood of our brave diocesan priests, the blood of the Jesuits massacred on November 16, 1989, the blood of more than eighty thousand Salvadorans killed for their faith in love. After all of these offerings there will be justice and there will be peace. Men and women, boys and girls of good will on Earth should work together so that this peace matures through hope, in faith, so that it produces the sweet fruit of love.

From one Eucharist to another—from March 20, 1977, to March 24, 1980—Monsignor Romero became an act of grace that symbolizes for our people the living flame that justifies the struggle of Christians and non-Christians for a better world. Romero thus lived in continual liturgy, illuminated by his prophetic word, in an attitude of giving. It that way he became the manifestation of God's glory among us, to live, in death, in the memory of the people and in the glory of God.

*Chapter 16*

# My Last Days in El Salvador

### Growing Fear and Departure from Suchitoto

FROM FEBRUARY 1977, I could not sleep at home because of the danger of being surprised by an assassin's hand. I did not want night to begin; I was afraid of the dark. After eight o'clock I looked for a place to sleep. Sometimes I stayed in the sacristy, other times in some friend's home; very often the Dominican sisters of Suchitoto's girls school opened their doors to me. The mother superior, a Nicaraguan, was very kind to me and gave me protection. Early the next morning, I was back at the parish house to celebrate the six o'clock mass.

The situation was oppressive and destructive to my nervous system. I knew it well: one's strength is exhausted, worry is constant, enemy attacks come one after another; in the end one suffers from what some call psychosomatic fear. This fear is when the rational yields to the irrational; one sees a policeman and tries to get away from him, a military uniform is a symbol of danger, the wind hitting a branch means someone's unwanted presence. Ultimately, sensitivity to danger blindly grows until one is in danger of falling victim to one's imaginary fears.

After the February 28, 1977, massacre in La Plaza Libertad, I returned home to Suchitoto. I thought I could still continue my work there. But in early March my sister Raquel arrived at my house with a note from Monsignor Romero, in which he instructed me to leave the city at once, assuring me that he would later explain why. My sister said, "Monsignor called the house very worried, something serious must be in store for you. He said you should not use your own vehicle."

I was familiar with these situations and knew I could not take my time and wait. Right away I went to see my neighbor, Ricardo Leiva, one of my best friends in town, and I told him what was happening. He said, "Let me call Hernández, an engineer in Santa Ana; he is building some silos for the Institute for Regulation of Supplies (IRA). If he allows it, you can leave in one of the closed trucks that are hauling in construction materials." Hernández, a Christian Democrat, was then the mayor of Santa Ana. I knew him well because he had done the cursillos de Cristiandad with me. Ricardo hung up the phone and said, "Wait for me a bit. I will be right back; I am going to the construction site." Ten minutes later he was back, followed by the driver of a huge eighteen-wheeler. As the order was to leave immediately, I took nothing with me.

At the entrance of San Martín there were three pairs of Guards checking vehicles coming from Suchitoto. As expected, they stopped us. I was next to my sister, right up close to her, my head covered with a hat. The guards took a brief look in the cab and asked if anyone was hidden in the back of the truck. The driver calmly answered no, then added, "I cannot lie to you, I was the bodyguard of Señor Regalado Dueñas who was assassinated; you remember him?" They said yes, they did, and signaled him to continue on. Once we arrived at the seminary, my final destination, the driver told me about himself and what had happened to him. That was my farewell to Suchitoto. From then on I lived at the San José de la Montaña Seminary, on the advice of Monsignor Romero.

I had arrived in Suchitoto at the end of 1968, after my studies in Ecuador. The persecution began in April of the following year and did not end until I left my country on May 25, 1977. I had remained at my post thanks to Monsignor Chávez y González's unconditional support and the immeasurable courage of my people, the campesinos, as well as some individuals in the city.

Eight years had passed. During that long time I learned that the struggle for a people's liberation is not easy; it brings continual problems. This is something one must accept beforehand so as not to embitter one's life or nourish hate in one's heart. In this way one lives joyfully during life's difficult and sad moments and rejoices in the triumphs, when the cause of freedom advances for the entire nation's benefit. The latter, "the whole nation," is essential and important, because we do not wish evil on the wealthy or those in power, but rather that everyone has a fair share under the law of the one over us, who created us, and who often does not agree with lawyers' laws or representatives' legislation.

Governments speak of respect for a country's laws to maintain national security. However, law is not always the same thing as legality. Legality is based on the very essence of a thing, while the law in most cases serves only certain groups' interests. Legality is born of our obligation to protect life, human rights, and nature. When legislators make laws, they often favor the interests of the population's dominant groups. As a result, we sometimes have laws that, in the name of national security, openly contradict the people's security.

One who is part of this people and on the same level of the people should experience the insecurity of the majority in order to build a new peaceful order. Is it possible this new order will arrive? Yes, but not completely, while man is man and woman is woman, pilgrims on this earth.

The Priests' Seminary of San Salvador, San José de la Montaña
Chencho Alas studied there from 1948 to 1955
Photo: Archives from Equipo Maíz

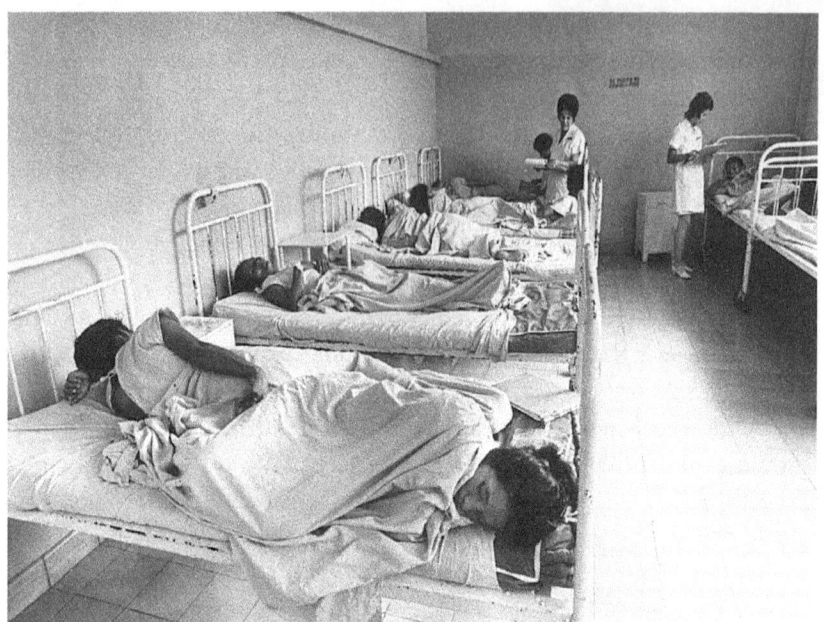

Women often sleep back to back in Suchitoto's maternity hospital
Photo: Cornell Capa (1972)
International Center of Photography, NY City

## Departure of Alfonso Navarro

Alfonso was one of the young priests of the San Salvador archdiocese. His priestly exercise lasted just ten years, from 1967 to 1977. He was loved by all of us, his compañeros. We all admired his cheerfulness, his *joie de vivre*, his creative spirit, and his deep sense of solidarity for those who suffered pain or poverty.

His first test as a man of new ideas came when he joined a group of seven of us who had organized to denounce the naming of Monsignor Mario Casariego, archbishop of Guatemala, as cardinal. Once Central American newspapers picked up the news published by the Vatican, Casariego wanted to proclaim himself cardinal of the region. In fact, his election was *in pectore*, which means it was an honor the Pope gave him as a person, as an individual. We all knew the sad history of this cleric's staunch alliance with the military, particularly General Maximiliano Hernández Martínez and the oligarchy. It was therefore worthwhile to denounce his efforts to tie himself to the wings of power and to anchor him instead to what he truly was: a brown-noser. In so doing, we were not only doing the church a favor, but also the bishops.

On April 22, 1969, our protest group published our manifesto, which I was tasked with writing, and it became the first special edition of *El Diario El Mundo*. It was also aired by *Radio Vaticana*, *La Voz de las Américas*, and the BBC of London. I was the oldest of the group. My friendship with Alfonso began there.

The military, as we say, had it out for Alfonso. As parish priest of Opico, he and his compañero, Father Guillermo "Garo" Rodriguez, were accused of organizing the campesinos against the landowners. Later, on May 27, 1971, Alfonso was accused by the country's press of protecting the kidnappers and murderers of Ernesto Regalado Dueñas, a descendant of the country's two richest families. The accusation was based on declarations made by Carlos Solórzano, who five days after having been seized by plainclothes police and disappeared was presented to the press saying that maybe Alfonso had helped those implicated in the killing, a group of university students, escape or hide. Such statements had no value, because everyone knew they were extracted by torture.

Alfonso taught religion at the Guadalupana High School. It was a private school, directed by women religious, and attended by daughters of the country's middle-and upper-class families. In all schools, there was a true Christian and social opening, a greater commitment to the Church's new teachings, and therefore men such as Alfonso were accepted as teachers. That did not mean all the students felt open to the new winds blowing in the Church. Among these young women, there were some who were totally opposed to the Christian opening of service to the poor. Apparently, one of them, the daughter of a senior military officer, was recording Alfonso's classes, something he was aware of, and the reason why Velarde Figueroa had summoned him to answer for his teachings. In our country, the military have granted themselves the intellectual capacity to judge whether or not a doctrine is Catholic, whether it adheres to the Church's teachings or is contrary to them.

A few weeks before his death, Alfonso again attracted his enemies' ire. On February 27, 1977, a week after the presidential elections, the most fraudulent in the country's history, Alfonso was invited to celebrate mass in the Plaza Libertad for the demonstrators who had taken the plaza indefinitely to protest the elections. Alfonso, aware that the archbishop's permission was needed to celebrate the Eucharist in public places, asked those inviting him to obtain the permit. Apparently, they got it, and Alfonso celebrated the eight o'clock evening mass. The plaza was filled with about ten thousand people. Alfonso left the event; in the early morning of February 28, armored trucks and troops appeared to clear the Plaza Libertad with bullets and machetes. Many died that night.

On May 11, 1977, at about two in the afternoon, Alfonso came to my room located on the second floor of San José de la Montaña Seminary. He looked worried, nervous. Without further ado he told me he had been summoned to a meeting with Colonel Velarde Figueroa, Molina's private secretary. Alfonso said, "You have spoken with people like this at different times. You know how to deal with them; advise me."

I tried to advise Alfonso, making him see that one must use direct and authoritarian language with the military, because that is what they understand. Their mind is structured to command and obey. You must insist with them that a priest, like a soldier, is obliged to follow his superiors' teachings, in this case those of the bishops and the messages of the Second Vatican Council and Medellín.

I do not know if my words helped my friend in some way. The truth is that from there he left for the presidential house. When the meeting was over, he passed by my room after speaking with Monsignor Rivera Damas to thank me for my advice and to say he had to leave immediately for his parish, located five minutes from the seminary, because he had a mass at the Divine Providence Hospital. That was the last time I spoke with Alfonso Navarro. Once the mass was over, he returned home, where several young people awaited him. Young people admired and followed him because he gave them support, advice, and an example of love of life.

Alfonso's only brother detailed what happened next in his small book titled *Testimonio*, from which I have taken the following quote:

> He arrived at the parish house around six in the afternoon and found several of his young friends reading and solving crossword puzzles in the living room. He greeted them and went to change clothes. Meanwhile, his friends left to go to a nearby store; the only one who stayed behind was his youngest visitor, Luisito Torres, fourteen years old. Alfonso picked up the newspaper he had borrowed, because he did not buy the *Diario de Hoy*, and he sat down to read it in an aluminum chair in the interior garden; the telephone rang, and he said to Luisito, "I will answer it." On hearing his voice, they hung up; he returned to the garden and again began

to read. Luisito remained in the living room. Almost immediately four men arrived at the front door and knocked softly.

Luisito went to open the door for them; they covered his mouth, turned his head. They put his face to the floor and pointed a gun at him from behind. They made masks of their handkerchiefs. One quickly went to the kitchen, grabbed the maid from behind, put a pistol to her neck and asked where the priest was; she said nothing. The other two looked in the rest of the rooms. At the sounds, Father Navarro rose from his chair and looked through the door to the garden. Seeing what was going on, he asked, "Please, what are you doing?" The one who had seized the young woman released her and ran to the priest. He gave him a karate kick that broke his forearm, threw him against the wall and floor, then began to shoot him. The other two ran to the door, and only one other was also able to shoot. Between the two, they unloaded seven 9-mm bullets into his body, one after the other. Lastly, one went to the priest's body and kicked him with contempt. They went to the door facing the street, and one last shot was heard: not to leave without killing, the hatchet man who held Luisito Torres turned his face and shot him in the forehead.[1]

"Fatally wounded," his brother added, "Alfonso called his young friends and said his farewells to them." His last words, on the way to the emergency room, were: "I know who has killed me, but I also want them to know I forgive them!" In accordance to his wishes, he was buried in his parish's chapel. The archdiocesan clergy had in Alfonso their first martyr.

Monsignor Óscar Romero, who was also living in the seminary since being named Archbishop of San Salvador, came to my room and gave me the news, almost crying. I remember his words: "This is very terrible, Chencho, and they are not going to stop. There are two dead, Rutilio and now Alfonso."

That very night, Father Francisco Estrada, provincial leader of the Jesuits, and Father Amando López, SJ, came looking for me. That was the second time Father López had been concerned for my safety. The first time was in Suchitoto, when he once arrived to secret me out of the city. Later, on November 16, 1989, Amando and five of his Jesuit compañeros were murdered by the army.

On that night in 1977, Francisco and Amando told me: "We consider it dangerous for you and the seminarians for you to live here any longer. They can come here to kill you and they can do much harm to others. It is better

1. Navarro, Napoleón. *Testimonio*, Publicación Búsqueda, 38–39.

that you leave the seminary and perhaps go to an embassy." I asked them to advise me where to go. It occurred to them that the best place might be the *nunciatura*, if the nuncio accepted me. In truth, I had no confidence in the nuncio; I was not a bird of his liking. I asked Estrada to call him and he did. That same night the two priests accompanied me to the Vatican Embassy.

The embassy is a good place for someone who has duties to perform, but not for a person taking refuge in it. True, I could have dedicated myself to reading books, but there was not anything else to do. By the second day I felt I had entered a tomb, and I quickly decided to call Monsignor Romero so that he could enlighten me on the decision to make. I certainly did not intend to stay in such a place. Monsignor arrived, accompanied by Monsignor Rivera Damas. After I described my new situation, he promised to visit President Molina to ask about my safety. Molina told him very clearly that he could offer me no protection, and it was better that I leave the country to avoid my death.

Two weeks later, the same nuncio took me to an airplane without going through normal procedures. He boarded the plane with me and once he saw me seated, he left. I thought my departure from the country would last only three months. It was not to be; it lasted fifteen years instead. I must confess that this was one of the most difficult experiences of my life. My departure was on May 25, 1977.

*Chapter 17*

# Thirty Years Later

## Exile

It has been thirty years since my arrival in Suchitoto. Many years have passed under the bridge of my life since then. During my years of exile, which began May 25, 1977, I have lived in the United States and Nicaragua. In the latter country, which I carry close to my heart, I resided for nine years. I learned a lot about the good and the bad of the Nicaraguan revolution. The first years of Sandinista life were glorious. I particularly remember the famous educational crusade across the entire nation, in which thousands upon thousands of young people participated to teach reading and writing to those who did not know how.

But I also remember the infamous "piñata," the distribution of state assets by corrupt Sandinistas after the electoral victory of the widow Doña Violeta de Chamorro; man reverted to acting the beast and forgot the ideals for which he had struggled. Of course, not everyone participated in that degrading exercise in greed.

Of the United States I remember many beautiful and good things, such as the support I have received, particularly from Jewish families, for projects in Nicaragua and especially in El Salvador. But I also remember the treatment given me by the American director of the Inter-American Development Bank during the Reagan era. He, along with the CIA, accused me of being the principal arms buyer for the FMLN in the United States. I am no friend of weapons. I think with each one produced, we become more inimical to our planet and further impoverish our people.

## Land, Liberation, and Death Squads

After twelve years of war, from 1980 to 1992, the Salvadoran government and the FMLN signed the Peace Accords. The Castle of Chapultepec in Mexico was elegantly dressed up for the signing of the peace. In El Salvador people celebrated the Accords' signing with parties. Everybody gave one another a peace hug. The word "brother" echoed in many throats. The celebration was our people's shout of hope; they did not want to see their children's blood run any longer. However, the violence continues! A campesino told me a while ago, "During the war we fought because we had a cause; now we have none. There is no reason for us to attack one another."

**Contradictions: Shantytown of Tutunichapa and the Jesuits' School**
Photo: Cornell Capa (1972)
International Center of Photography, NY City

# THIRTY YEARS LATER

Homeless person
Photo: Cornell Capa (1972)
International Center of Photography, NY City

## Something Must Be Done

With the signing of the Accords, I could, after fifteen years in exile, return to my country. Since then, a question has swirled in my mind: And *now*, what can I do for my country? When one reads reports stating that every day on average one police officer is violently killed, that there are more deaths now than during the war years, and that violence consumes 13 percent of the gross domestic product, a rate five times higher than the country's annual growth, one trembles with rage and anguish.

The people surely are not being given an answer. If the prewar years are compared with the postwar, wealth is more concentrated nowadays. The elite have played dirty with the country. With a laurel wreath on his head, the former president who signed the peace accord now devotes himself to signing checks that allow him to enjoy much of the country's wealth. He did not privatize the national bank for nothing, after all.

Several FMLN politicians have grown comfortable in government posts and have forgotten the ideals for which they fought. They are interested in government work for the juicy pay they receive; they care very little about the situation in which the people live. Policies are designed to favor the financial sector, forgetting the countryside, which employs the majority of our people. For the latest example of these policies we have the county's "dollarization"; since January 2001 the American dollar has been adopted as the national currency, which has practically eliminated the Salvadoran colón.

Something must be done. We cannot cross our arms and hope that others will solve our problems. Each can contribute a little or a lot, but certainly something, to create an environment in which humans get along. For me, I think my contribution is to work with the Coordinating Committee of the Bajo Lempa and the Bay of Jiquilisco to establish its project of a Local Peace Zone. After having worked to apply the principles of liberation theology in Suchitoto, it seems that for this period in our country's history, I should work in what could be called a theology of peace. It is logical.

In our culture of criminal violence, it is necessary to establish the values, principles, and attitudes of a culture of peace. The violence in the country has very deep, intertwined roots. There has been no political will to establish a doctrine of democratic security that would allow for the creation of the instruments needed to bring about a peace culture. The population is armed to the teeth, the justice system is weak, and public security lacks the means to ensure order. Although there is much talk of eradicating poverty, more is spent on paper and ink than on what is done. The churches are absent from the population's great problems. All this, and many other things indicate that we have not yet responded to the commitment to peace, that we are very far from complying with Jesus's beatitude: "Blessed are the peacemakers, for they will be called children of God" (Matt. 5:9).

## Communities of the Bajo Lempa

In the Bajo Lempa region, we have begun this hard work of peacemaking. Slowly, we are attempting to enact a theology of peace that will help the communities in the area move forward. In the 1980s, this part of El Salvador, the south of Usulután, was an area of conflict and sometimes the theater of war. Prior to the signing of the Peace Accords, in 1992, and for a while after, ex-combatants of the FMLN and of the government settled in this area, along with refugees who returned from Panama, Costa Rica, Nicaragua, and Honduras. In addition, there was a small number who had not left their homes. Most of this population suffers flooding year after year, caused in part by excessive rain and lack of drainage canals, and especially by the CEL each time it opens the floodgates of the Quince de Septiembre hydroelectric dam. Upriver, CEL has built five dams, making the Lempa both the country's major source of energy and of disasters.

In October 1995, there was a great flood that affected some ten thousand inhabitants, who had to be evacuated from their communities. As expected, they lost their crops, most of their animals, and some of their houses. This sounded the warning bell for this region. At that time, the Institute of Technology, Self-Management, and Environment (ITAMA) and several other NGOs lent their technical and administrative services. Leaders of affected communities approached ITAMA and requested advice in solving the flooding problem, or at least to learn to live with it.

As a result of this process, seven communities agreed to form the Coordinating Committee of Lower Lempa Communities for the Prevention of Disasters. As its first activity they decided to go to the Legislative Assembly and ask that the region be declared a disaster zone, which they accomplished. CEL committed to communicating with them in advance whenever the floodgates were to be opened, and they provided them with three radios. Unfortunately CEL has no early warning system allowing two or three days' notice before it discharges water. At best, they can communicate four hours in advance.

The following year, the Coordinating Committee decided to include sustainable economic development as a new objective. What was important about this objective was that it allowed for the training of families in clean agricultural techniques that would not pollute soil, water, or air. The greatest fruit of this project was the increase in the number of communities that decided to become part of the Coordinating Committee, and therefore to work together to analyze sustainable development alternatives.

## Local Peace Zone

That same year, 1996, Ramón López Reyes visited El Salvador. I met Ramón in Dublin, Ireland, in the mid-1980s, during a conference on the relationship between weapons production and poverty, to which I was invited to give a lecture. On that occasion we discussed the need to establish a peace center in El Salvador, once the war ended. López Reyes, an ex-colonel from the United States, a warrior converted to the struggle for peace, is the founder and director of the International Center for the Study and Promotion of Zones of Peace in the World, with headquarters in Hawaii.

With the help of Ramón López Reyes, Dr. Fabio Castillo, and Mario López, now dead, we established in the south of Usulután the first Local Zone of Peace in Latin America and probably the world. My contribution has been to give almost all the workshops about the Local Zone of Peace, thirty-five in all.

Currently, the Local Zone of Peace project represents the framework and ultimate objective of the various programs of the Coordinating Committee of the Lower Lempa and the Bay of Jiquilisco, which is defined as an independent, autonomous social movement. Our project encompasses human rights and responsibilities; the solution, transformation, or mediation of conflicts; democratic participation; and sustainable economic development. In the workshops I have given I have added to each of these peacemaking pillars a theological vision, which I consider necessary. Work done with a conscience is more effective and permanent.

After thirty years of having begun pastoral work in Suchitoto that put land tenure at the center of social interests, I think it is good to contribute now in another historical circumstance involving the fate of Usulután's campesinos. Rather than raise funds for projects, I think my greatest contribution is directed to what could be considered a theology of peace in the local peace zone.

## The Poor of Suchitoto and the Third World

The facts narrated in this work's previous chapters illustrate the poor's own ideas. They speak to us of the reality in which Suchitoto's poor have lived and continue to live, of their struggles and hopes. They speak to us of how they managed to raise their awareness of their own situation and of their willingness to change, which led them not only to organize but also to fight for social demands and to participate in politics. It was truly a process that unfolded; it began with evangelization, continued into social demands, and eventually led to the political arena. This process was not planned in advance; it was not born of a blueprint for future transformation. It evolved naturally, by the same dynamics of analysis and ideas with which they were dealing, and compelled by the changing reality they were approaching. They had no Marxist manual in front of them, which they had to follow, nor a Cuban advisor, an expert in subversive techniques, as the genocidal cynic Ronald Reagan imagined.

In its time, Suchitoto's contribution constituted a grain to the construction of a new vision of pastoral work in El Salvador. In other parishes in the beginning of the 1970s a similar renovation was also carried out following the teachings of the Second Vatican Council, of Medellín, and applications elaborated during the first National Week of Pastoral Work. I think it would be good for men such as David Rodríguez, Rafael Barahona, Tilo Sánchez, Ricardo Ayala, Roberto Trejos, and others to put their memories in writing. Certainly the diocesan clergy was the initiator of the big changes in the country, thanks largely to archbishops Luis Chávez y González, Arturo Rivera Damas, and Óscar Romero. The clergy belonging to religious orders, especially the Jesuits, later joined this effort, and their impact on our society has been invaluable in practice and in the intellectual field. The work of political, economic, and social analysis of the Simeón Cañas University has been of the highest order. They should continue it, because history does not stand still.

The poor of Suchitoto, of El Salvador, of Latin America, of the Third World, are those without land, who rent or sharecrop the worst land, the eroded land, because the good land is dedicated to coffee, to cotton, to sugarcane, to cattle. In a word, to export crops that produce foreign currency, which remains in the banks of the countries to the north.

The poor are those without homes, who live in shantytowns in the cities or shacks in the countryside. They are those who eat twice a day, sometimes beans and rice, or only beans and tortillas, and sometimes merely tortillas with salt, chile, and lemon. They are those who arrive at two in the morning to line up at the Rosales Hospital to be seen in the afternoon or simply are not served. If they are hospitalized, they are crowded together in beds in hospitals that have no medicines and not even bed sheets. So often in Suchitoto I saw women who had just given birth, lying in pairs in those narrow beds!

The poor are our children who come to school faint, without having eaten breakfast because there is no food at home, with their rags torn or all patched and without having bathed, because running water in the house is a luxury for the "middle class."

The poor are women subjected by religion to endless procreation in marriage. The women are those who constantly listen to many voices: "Mommy, I want water, I want food, I want clothes, I hurt myself, I want to play." And to top it off, they are slapped around by drunken husbands and get dirty looks from those who sell pork rind in the market.

These oppressed poor, who represent the majority of the planet's population, belong, in a very high proportion, to countries dependent on the rich and exploitative North. This reality of the poor and poverty, of dependent countries, has always existed; it is not new. What is new is the awareness of the situation, a consciousness that makes the poor break into present-day history with plans for liberation. Some within the Church have committed themselves to listening to these plans from those able of opening dialogue with the poor. Their reflections in the light of revelation represent a new way of doing theology. This new way from Latin America is called liberation theology. Its foundation rests upon the poor who have gained awareness and on the person of Jesus as found in the Bible. We find these two elements in rich exchange in Christian Base Communities. In these groups, theology is done with the same rights, obligations, and wisdom as in a university classroom.

If our ministry in Suchitoto had not had the land struggle ingredient, it would have still been on the cutting edge within the church, but it would not have had wider repercussions. Perhaps they would have admired us in church circles, or condemned us, for having been the first to introduce Christian Base Communities; for having organized a body of Celebrants of the Word prepared during two-month courses every year; for having been the first in the country and probably in Central America to concede power to laypersons, in our case to campesinos, so that they could give communion; for having celebrated the mass with tortillas and coffee, something theologically correct; or for having initiated talks to teach parents the meaning of their children's baptism. Truly, we were pioneers in pastoral ministry. Nevertheless, that was not all. I would say what was most important about our work was in uniting, for the first time in the country, pastoral ministry with social and political life, believing that pastoral work without social and political dimensions is disembodied, that it lacks flesh and bones, that it is not incarnated in the community or country. It would be the same if we deleted the beatitudes from the Gospel, or the passage of Luke 4:18–21, in which Jesus discloses his mission, or even worse, Matthew 25:31–46, which reveals what will happen in the final judgment.

Sometimes I think, reflecting on the church in my country, there are times when cowardice is disguised as prudence, in open contradiction to the Gospel of Jesus. This cannot be. We need the fresh and inspiring breeze of the Second Vatican Council that the good Pope John XXIII gave us; the dedication, courage, and devotion of many of our parishes' campesinos, some of whom are now our martyrs; the prophetic message of priests who died at the altar, in their places of work or rest; the generosity of patricians like Enrique Álvarez Córdova who understood one can be rich while sharing with the poor; our young students' dream of a better country; the courage of our worker martyrs; and especially the light of Monsignor Romero who, like Jesus, gave light to the blind and hope to the oppressed.

Our country needs spirituality that gives life to the material, and peace that affords us the necessary harmony for body and soul, at the individual and community level, in a political, economic, social, cultural, and ecological environment, good and beautiful. Our country needs to return to the goodness God imprinted on his creation, according to the first chapter of Genesis, the beauty of which our Mayan ancestors spoke. We have lost that beauty and goodness to crime, which cripples the human body and subjects nature to an equally horrific destruction. We are hopelessly dehumanizing ourselves. Perhaps the campesinos of Lower Lempa organized in the local peace zone will return to us the hope that each day becomes more and more distant.

# Bibliography

Alas, Higinio. *Domesticacíon escolar y alternativa: Una autoeducación antropologica comunitaria.* San Jose, Costa Rica: EDUCA, 1979.

Cabarrús, Carlos Rafael. *Génesis de una revolución: Analisis del surgimiento y desarrollo de la organización campesina en El Salvador.* Ediciones de la Casa Chata. Mexico City: Centro de Investigaciones y Estudios Superiores en Anthropologia Social, 1983.

Ellacuría, Ignacio. "La historización del concepto de propiedad como principio de desideologización." In *Veinte años de historia en El Salvador (1969–1989): Escritos políticos*, Tomo 1, San Salvador: UCA Editores, 1991, 595.

———. "A sus órdenes, mi capital." In *Veinte años de historia en El Salvador (1969–1989): Escritos políticos*, Tomo 1, San Salvador: UCA Editores, 1991, 649–656.

Gould, Jeffrey and Aldo L. Lauria-Santiago. *To Rise in Darkness: Revolution, Repression, and Memory in El Salvador, 1920–1932.* Durham, NC: Duke University Press, 2008.

Hoeffel, Paul Heath. "Eclipse of the Oligarchs." In *The New York Times Magazine*, September 6, 1981, http://www.nytimes.com/1981/09/06/magazine/the-eclipse-of-the-oligarchs.html?pagewanted=all.

Latin American Episcopal Conference (CELAM). "Medellín Documents: Justice." September 6, 1968. http://www.shc.edu/theolibrary/resources/medjust.htm.

Masferrer, Alberto. "El minimum vital," Originally written in 1929. In *Cultura: Revista de Ministerio del Educación* 47, special edition "Un homenaje a Don Alberto Masferrer," (January-March 1968), pp. 117–132.

Navarro, Napoleón. *Testimonio,* San Salvador, El Salvador, Publicación Búsqueda , 1978, 38–39.

Pope Paul VI. *Gaudium et Spes.* December 7, 1965. http://www.vatican.va/archive/hist_councils/ii_vatican_council/documents/vat-ii_cons_19651207_gaudium-et-spes_en.html.

Romero, Oscar and Arturo Rivera Damas. "The Church and Popular Political Organizations." Third Pastoral Letter, August 6, 1978.

www.ingramcontent.com/pod-product-compliance
Lightning Source LLC
Chambersburg PA
CBHW071444150426
43191CB00008B/1231